Fusion \`fyű zhən\ n.:

a merging of diverse, distinct, or separate elements into a unified whole

Food \ füd \ n. :

a theme throughout Scripture

by Eric Rottm

CONCORDIA PUBLISHING HOUSE · SAINT LOUIS

3558 S. Jefferson Ave., St. Louis, MO 63118–3968
1–800–325–3040 • www.cph.org

Written by Erik Rottmann
Edited by Mark S. Sengele
Designed by Karol Bailey

This publication may be available in braille, in large print, or on cassette tape for the visually impaired. Please allow 8 to 12 weeks for delivery. Write to the Library for the Blind, 7550 Watson Rd., St. Louis, MO 63119–4409; call toll-free 1–888–215–2455; or visit the Web site: www.blindmission.org.

Your comments and suggestions concerning the material are appreciated. Please write the Editor of Youth Materials, Concordia Publishing House, 3558 S. Jefferson Avenue, St. Louis, MO 63118–3968.

Manufactured in the United States of America

1 2 3 4 5 6 7 8 9 10 15 14 13 12 11 10 09 08 07 06

Table of Contents

INTRODUCTION

About the Fusion Series

Fusion—the merging of diverse, distinct, or separate elements into a unified whole. *Fusion* is a word that speaks of energy and excitement, whether you are talking about a style of music or a nuclear reaction.

God's Word is filled with fusion. The Old Testament bears many hints of events to come in the New Testament, yet we often miss the connection. The Gospel message of the Savior is seen time and again in the Old Testament. Through this series you will come to connect—fuse—those events and messages for yourself and your participants.

Each study in the Fusion Series gathers stories from Scripture—both Old and New Testaments—around a common theme. Our prayer is that, through the study of that theme, you will come to a deeper understanding of the Gospel message of Jesus Christ as Lord and Savior.

Fusion—Food

Throughout His Old Testament, God repeatedly connects food to His acts of salvation. During the exodus from Egypt, God gave the Passover meal to His people Israel. He daily supplied them with manna and quail during their wilderness journey, until that great day they entered the land He had promised them. Even then, God continued to provide for His people by means of Canaan's bounty. God also used special food to provide for King David, for Daniel, and for Elijah during their times of struggle. In so doing, God sustained and strengthened each of them when other comforts failed. As shown by the Gospel of Matthew, food likewise figures prominently in New Testament themes of forgiveness and salvation. Revelation also features food in its message of forgiveness, depicting a future meal of fulfillment at which God's saints will find satisfaction for their "hunger and thirst for righteousness" (Matthew 5:6). These occurrences of food joined to salvation in the Scriptures will lead the class participants into greater understanding and rejoicing in the meal of Holy Communion, through which God continues to join His people to salvation even to this day.

Using These Materials

Fusion Series Bible studies are designed to challenge your participants to develop a deeper knowledge and understanding of Scripture. These studies work for either large-group presentation or small-group Bible study. While there are six sessions outlined in the book, there are no suggested time limits for each section of the lesson. The level of participant interest, discussion, and further questions will help establish the length of time to spend on each section. This flexibility also allows you to use this material for more than six one-hour sessions. You can easily adapt this material to twelve or more hour-long lessons.

Each session contains reproducible participant pages. These pages may be given to participants as you work through the lesson together in class. As an alternative, you may give copies of these pages to participants in advance of the session so that they may complete their personal study before coming to class.

The leader's materials work through the questions from the participant pages and provide additional commentary and insights for the Bible class leader. You will want to study these notes as you prepare to lead each session.

It is assumed that the Bible class leader will have the usual basic equipment and supplies available—pencils or pens for each participant and a chalkboard or its equivalent (white board, overhead transparency projector, or newsprint pad and easel) with corresponding markers or chalk. Encourage the participants to bring their own Bibles. Then they can mark useful passages and make notes to guide their personal Bible study and reference. Do provide additional Bibles, however, for visitors or participants who do not bring one. The appropriate participant pages should be copied in a quantity sufficient for the class.

1

In Remembrance of Me

The Passover Meal

Lesson Focus

The Passover meal plays a central role in Israel's exodus from the bondage of Egypt. The Passover lamb not only nourished God's people for their journey into the wilderness, but the lamb's blood also provided them with protection and safety from God's avenging angel. Israel's annual celebration of the Passover later set the stage for the Last Supper, in which Christ gives His Church a new meal of salvation. St. Paul uses the Passover to describe the salvation that is now ours in Christ. He declares, "Christ, our Passover Lamb, has been sacrificed" (1 Corinthians 5:7).

Introduction

Ask students, "What memories come to mind for you when you think about certain foods, such as a peanut butter-and-jelly sandwich or green gelatin?" Foods are often very strongly associated with memories. A peanut butter-and-jelly sandwich may remind you of your childhood, while green gelatin may remind you of many church potluck dinners. When you eat such foods, your thoughts are immediately transported to those other times, people, and memories with which you associate these foods.

Now "amplify" your understanding of memory to be something more than recalling past events. Think about remembrance in the way the Bible uses the word—as a way of allowing God's people to participate in events that took place long before they were born. This will shed light on Jesus' words concerning Holy Communion, "Do this in remembrance of Me" (Luke 22:19).

In the Old Testament, God gave His people the Passover meal. In the New Testament, He gives His people the meal of Holy Communion. Both of these meals have strong memories attached—memories of God's great acts of salvation. Even though the people who ate the Passover meal in the Old Testament might not have actually participated in the exodus, their eating this meal joined them to that great event. In the same way, God's followers eat the Lord's Supper as a way of not merely remembering a story, but actually participating in the death and resurrection of Jesus Christ for their salvation.

Opening Prayer

It is truly good, right, and salutary that we should at all times and in all places give thanks to You, holy Lord, almighty Father, everlasting God. You bid Your people cleanse their hearts and prepare with joy for the paschal feast. Renew our zeal in faith and life, and bring us to the fullness of grace that belongs to the children of God. Therefore with angels and archangels and with all the company of heaven we laud and magnify Your glorious name, evermore praising You and saying: Holy, holy, holy Lord, God of Sabaoth. Heaven and earth are full of Your glory. Hosanna in the highest. Blessed is He who comes in the name of the Lord. Hosanna in the highest. Amen. (Preface for Lent, LW, pp. 147, 148–49)

Setting the Scene

Read Genesis 41:53–42:5. What first caused the family of Israel to visit Egypt? Who was already there, keeping charge of Egypt's grain storage? How is it that he ended up in such a powerful position? (To review the story, check Genesis 37:26–28; 39; 41:25–45.)

In keeping with Pharaoh's prophetic dreams (see Genesis 41:25–36), the land of Egypt enjoyed seven years of plenty followed by seven years of famine. This devastating famine extended beyond Egypt and spread "over all the earth" (Genesis 41:57), including the land of Canaan. When Jacob (a.k.a. Israel) learned that Egypt had grain available for sale, he said to his ten elder sons, "Go down and buy grain for us there, that we may live and not die" (Genesis 42:2). Both Jacob and his sons were unaware that Joseph, having survived slavery and imprisonment, had risen to the most important position in all Egypt, second only to Pharaoh himself. Because God enabled Joseph to interpret the meaning of the Pharaoh's disturbing dreams, Pharaoh placed Joseph in charge of storing up enough grain during the years of plenty to feed all of Egypt during the years of famine (Genesis 41:39–40).

In Genesis 50:19–21, what explanation does Joseph give his brothers concerning God's purpose for Joseph's years of slavery and imprisonment? Who, then, ultimately saved the family of Israel by providing them with food? See James 1:17.

Joseph refused to take any personal credit for saving Jacob and his entire family from starvation. Joseph pointed to God instead, who had allowed Joseph to suffer for so many years for the precise purpose of saving his family. Joseph promised, "I will provide for you and your little ones" (Genesis 50:21), but he first confessed, "God meant it for good, to bring it about that many people should be kept alive" (v. 20).

Joseph addressed his brothers with a wonderful question: "Am I in the place of God?" (Genesis 50:19). There is a sense in which this question could be answered as both yes and no. On one hand, the answer is no! This would be as if Joseph were saying, "I am not in the place of God. If God forgives you all your sins, who am I to hold them against you?"

But there is also a sense in which we could acknowledge that yes, Joseph is in the place of God. That is to say, God is providing for Joseph's family through Joseph! Joseph is the one who welcomed his family to Egypt, filled their bellies, and gave them a place to live, but ultimately God is the provider of all such good things. "Every good gift and every perfect gift [including the gifts that Joseph gave to his family] is from above, coming down from the Father of lights, with whom there is no variation or shadow due to change" (James 1:17).

Where did Jacob (a.k.a. Israel) and his family eventually move, according to Genesis 46:1–7? In what way does this set the stage for the exodus, according to Exodus 1:1–14?

Jacob and his family settled in the land of Egypt, in keeping with God's command. Just as Joseph had previously gone into this land as a way of saving many people (recall Genesis 50:19–21), so now the entire family of Israel goes into Egypt. This sets the stage for God's greatest act of salvation in the Old Testament—the exodus. While in Egypt, the people of Israel grew into a mighty nation. The Egyptians soon began to fear that Israel would become too numerous and powerful, so the new Pharaoh ordered that the Israelites be enslaved. Yet "the more they [the Israelites] were oppressed, the more they multiplied and the more they spread abroad" (Exodus 1:12)!

The Pharaoh refused to let God's people go, even after Egypt suffered nine horrible plagues. What tenth and final plague does God promise in Exodus 11:4–8? Who or what would be included in this plague, according to verse 5? In what way does this promise of destruction get fulfilled in Exodus 12:29–32?

In His most drastic measure to get Egypt to allow Israel to leave, God threatened to kill the firstborn of all the people and the cattle in the land. Because Pharaoh did not learn his lesson with the previous nine plagues, he still refused to let Israel leave. As a result of his continually hardened heart, the tenth plague descended upon Egypt just as Moses promised, killing even Pharaoh's own firstborn son (Exodus 12:29).

Before continuing with this important Old Testament story, study it from New Testament perspective. What does Jesus say about the Old Testament in John 5:39? In Luke 24:25–27, what resource does the resurrected Jesus use to teach His disciples while traveling on the road to Emmaus? What insight does Peter add in Acts 10:43?

In an earlier passage, John stated that the Jews wanted to kill Jesus, not only because He was breaking the Sabbath, but also because He called "God His own Father, making Himself equal with God" (John 5:18). Jesus responds by telling the Jews that, if they want to know about Him, they must "search the Scriptures," for "it is they that bear witness about Me" (John 5:39). When Jesus used the word *Scriptures* in this verse, He was speaking specifically about the Old Testament. The Old Testament was also Jesus' resource for instructing His disciples on the road to Emmaus the first Easter Sunday. "Beginning with Moses [i.e., the first five books of the Old Testament, called the Pentateuch] and all the Prophets, He interpreted to them in all the Scriptures the things concerning Himself" (Luke 24:27). Speaking along the same lines, Peter declared, "To Him [Jesus] all the prophets bear witness" (Acts 10:43).

These important passages from the New Testament alert us to the fact that the Old Testament Scriptures speak to us about God the Son, the long-awaited Jewish Messiah. Therefore, as we read stories such as the exodus, complete with its miraculous Passover meal, we must read them with Christ in mind. This is why Martin Luther, who specialized in teaching the Old Testament, could say, "The books of Moses and the prophets are Gospel too, since they first preached and wrote about Christ" (*What Luther Says,* no. 3150).

As will become clear in the next question, Paul bids us to pay particular attention to the Passover meal and its relationship to Christ.

What image does Paul use to describe Jesus in 1 Corinthians 5:7? How might this image influence the way you read Exodus 12:1–28, the story of the Passover?

Paul identifies an important link between Jesus Christ and the Old Testament Passover when he says, "Christ, our Passover lamb, has been sacrificed" (1 Corinthians 5:7). Realizing this connection, it would be fruitful to read the account of the Passover with Christ in mind, taking note of any details that both Christ and the Passover appear to have in common. This is what Martin Luther did, with the result that he preached the following stirring sermon comparing Christ with the Passover:

> *Look, then, upon our Paschal [Passover] Lamb, the Lord Christ. He wants to punish Pharaoh and all Egypt, that is, sin, death, and the devil, and free His Christian Church from their tyranny. Therefore He permits Himself, as the Paschal Lamb, to be killed and roasted on the tree of the cross that He may sprinkle us with His blood and that the angel of death, who had received power over us because of sin, should pass us by and do us no harm. Thus Paul well says, "Christ, our Passover, is sacrificed for us" (1 Corinthians 5:7), that is, sacrificed so that we are saved through His blood, and the devil, death, and sin should have no power over us nor do us any harm.* (What Luther Says, *no. 553)*

A Special Meal

Read about God's gift of the Passover meal in Exodus 12:1–28. As you read, keep a list of things that remind you—even in a small way—of Jesus, His work of salvation for you, and how that work of salvation gets distributed to you today.

Feel free to take a few minutes to briefly discuss the points of comparison that the students identified. Not all of these points may be directly applicable, but use their lists to encourage discussion. Points of comparison might include, but are not necessarily limited to the sacrificial lamb (v. 3); the blood on the doorposts (v. 7); the eating of the lamb (v. 8); the striking of the firstborn on account of rebellion and sin (v. 12); the keeping of the feast (v. 14); and the Lord providing protection from the destroyer by means of this meal (v. 23).

Then read and discuss this passage from seminary professor Adolph Harstad:

> *The Passover Feast was far more than food for the body. Instituted by the LORD Himself, it was a time of rich spiritual nourishment through food for the soul. The Passover celebration recalled the great release from Egypt. . . . Passover meant deliverance and redemption. Like the sparing of Israel and the exodus from bondage that it celebrated, it was a proof and seal of the LORD's resolve to rescue His people from all their foes (sin, death, and the devil as well as worldly enemies). Nothing could stop Him from fulfilling all His covenant promises. He had pushed aside a mighty pharaoh and the waters of the Red Sea so that He could keep His word to Abraham. In the fullness of time, He would redeem all humanity through the sacrifice of Jesus Christ, His true Passover Lamb.* (Joshua, *p. 240)*

What especially important characteristic must the Passover lamb have, according to Exodus 12:5? How does this compare to 1 Peter 1:18–19 and Hebrews 4:15?

The Passover lamb must be "without blemish" (Exodus 12:5). Using the same wording, Peter describes Jesus Christ as the "lamb without blemish or spot" (1 Peter 1:19). The perfect, blemish-free Passover lamb was a living representation of the sinless, perfect Jesus, who bore all of our sins and purchased our redemption. Yet Jesus' sinless perfection does not mean He was unaware of the ways we struggle with temptation and sin. Paul proclaims the assurance that "we do not have a high priest who is unable to sympathize with our weaknesses, but one who in every respect has been tempted as we are, yet without sin" (Hebrews 4:15).

Martin Luther once wrote a hymn titled "Death Held Our Lord in Prison," in which he beautifully developed the theme of Christ's Passover sacrifice for our salvation:

Here is the true Paschal Lamb
Which God himself attested.
That was on the tree of shame
In flaming passion roasted
His blood on our doorpost lies;
Faith holds that before Death's eyes;
The smiting angel can do nought. Alleluia! (*AE* 53:257)

(This same hymn has also been translated as "Christ Jesus Lay in Death's Strong Bands" [*LW* 123; *TLH* 195], but that translation does not make the point quite so well.)

What promise does God speak to His people in Exodus 12:7, 12–13? What does the shedding of blood indicate, according to Leviticus 17:11? From what did the shed blood of the Passover lamb and the other Old Testament sacrifices ultimately offer God's people protection? See Hebrews 9:22 and 1 John 1:7.

God promises that He will pass over the houses marked with blood on their doorposts, not sending the plague of death upon the people who live inside. Those who believed the Word of the Lord and painted the blood on their doorposts were saved. According to Leviticus 17:11, the shedding of blood indicates atonement for sins. The Passover lamb died in place of the people for whom it was sacrificed, protecting them not only from the last plague on Egypt (Exodus 12:13), but also from the death and judgment due to them because of their sins. In the same way, Christ the true Passover Lamb died in our place, atoning for our sins by paying the death penalty that was due to us.

Hebrews 9:22 warns, "Without the shedding of blood there is no forgiveness of sins." And 1 John 1:7 answers that blood has already been shed for our sake—the blood of Jesus, which "cleanses us from all sin."

What help does Hebrews 10:4 provide toward a right understanding of the Passover lamb and the other sacrifices of the Old Testament?

Hebrews 10:4 states, "It is impossible for the blood of bulls and goats to take away sins." The slain Passover lamb, along with the other blood sacrifices of the Old Testament, did not take away sin in and of themselves, but they were a living anticipation of the last, great sacrifice of God's Son. The Old Testament sacrifices provided God's people with a connection to the future sacrifice of Jesus on the cross, distributing to them the forgiveness that He would win for them in the future. Just as Holy Communion delivers Jesus' forgiveness, life, and salvation to New Testament believers, so the blood sacrifices delivered these same gifts to Old Testament believers.

Seminary professor David Scaer writes, "Important historical events in the Jewish community were commemorated with rituals that were not acts devoid of meaning; instead, they brought into the present what God had done for Israel in the past" (*Discourses in Matthew*, p. 176). According to these words, Israel's Passover celebration not only commemorated God's great act of salvation in the exodus from Egypt, but it also brought the exodus into the present. Even though a Passover lamb was sacrificed each year throughout Israel's history, this sacrifice was not a new sacrifice. Rather, it was a way that God had provided to connect all of His Israelites to the one great act of salvation in the exodus. In the same way, God's people today eat and drink Christ's body and blood in Holy Communion. Holy Communion brings God's greatest act of salvation—Christ's death and resurrection for sins—into the present. Holy Communion connects each participant to the history of salvation. "As in the Old Testament, a meal of liberation [that is, the Passover meal and the meal of Holy Communion] and the liberation itself comprise one event or reality" (*Discourses in Matthew,* p. 167).

The first Passover meal involved a sacrificial lamb whose blood was shed to protect the people from judgment. What were the people instructed to do with the lamb in Exodus 12:8? In what way is this verse significant, not only for Old Testament believers, but also for Christians today?

God instructed His people to eat the Passover lamb that had been slain for them. The very same body that had been sacrificed now was consumed in faith. In the same way, when Christians eat and drink Holy Communion, they receive Christ's body sacrificed for them and His blood shed for their salvation.

What additional foods were to be eaten with the Passover lamb, according to Exodus 12:8? What significance might these foods have had for the people of Israel? See Exodus 1:14 and Deuteronomy 16:3.

Along with the Passover lamb, God's people were also to eat unleavened bread and bitter herbs. Exodus 1:14 explains the bitter herbs: "[The Egyptians] made their lives bitter with hard service." By commemorating Passover with bitter herbs, God's people had a perpetual reminder of the bitter and harsh lives from which God graciously saved them. Deuteronomy 16:3 explains that the unleavened bread would remind the people of the haste by which they ate (see Exodus 12:11). This bread is also called "the bread of affliction" (Deuteronomy 16:3).

Unleavened bread (that is, bread without yeast) symbolizes haste in the Passover meal. What meaning does Jesus attach to yeast in Matthew 16:5–12? How does St. Paul speak about yeast in 1 Corinthians 5:6–8?

Jesus compares yeast to the false teaching of the Pharisees and Sadducees—those who rejected Jesus' words. Just as a small amount of yeast will quickly fill an entire loaf of bread, so also will false teachings quickly fill the hearts and minds of those who entertain and tolerate the false teachings. Jesus warns, "Beware."

In 1 Corinthians 5:6–8, St. Paul elaborates on Jesus' warning by saying, "a little leaven leavens the whole lump." Paul does not compare yeast to false teaching, but to boasting (v. 6), malice, and evil (v. 8). Yet Paul is not contradicting Jesus with these words. Boasting, malice and false teaching all are related sins in that they ignore God's Word for the sake of selfish opinions and desires.

Paul calls upon the Corinthians to "cleanse out the old leaven," that is, to repent of their proud and boastful ways. Using the imagery of the Passover feast, Paul points the Corinthians to the forgiveness that had been won for them by Christ: "For Christ, our Passover lamb, has been sacrificed. Let us therefore celebrate the festival, not with the old leaven, the leaven of malice and evil, but with the unleavened bread of sincerity and truth" (1 Corinthians 5:7–8).

Luther's hymn "Death Held Our Lord in Prison" speaks not only about the theme of the Passover lamb (see above), but also about the image of leaven or yeast.

We eat—and so we well fare—
Right Easter cakes sans leaven;
The old leaven shall not share
In the new word from heaven.
Christ himself will be the food,
Alone fill the soul with good:
Faith will live on nothing other. Alleluia! (*AE* 53:257)

In what way might these words from Jesus and from St. Paul add significance to the unleavened bread, especially in light of Exodus 12:19?

To celebrate the Passover rightly, God commanded that every Israelite home be carefully swept clean of all yeast. This requirement suggests that the absence of yeast, even in the Old Testament, signified something more than mere haste in leaving Egypt. God's people are required to put all yeast out of their homes, in a way very similar to Jesus' command that His disciples beware of—and avoid—the malicious false teaching of the Pharisees and Sadducees.

Take a look at Exodus 12:21–22. What sort of "paintbrush" were the people to use for putting the blood of the Passover lamb on the doorposts of their houses? King David also speaks about this plant in Psalm 51:7. What might David have had in mind as he prayed for forgiveness of his sins?

When David prays, "Purge me with hyssop, and I shall be clean" (Psalm 51:7), he jogs the reader's memory, bringing to mind that Israel used a hyssop "paintbrush" to mark their doorposts with the shed blood of the Passover lamb. Quite possibly, when David prayed for forgiveness of the sins that so relentlessly tortured him (see Psalm 51:3), he had in mind the sacrificial lamb who protected God's people from death. Now, confronted by the thought of God's judgment, David yearned to have the same protection from divine wrath as Israel enjoyed in the exodus.

God attaches a promise to His Passover meal (Exodus 12:13), but He also attaches a command to it. See Exodus 12:14–20. What did God command Israel concerning this meal? What punishments does He give for those who do not take the meal seriously and eat in a way that is contrary to the way God has commanded?

God required Israel to observe the Passover as a feast to the Lord "throughout your generations" (Exodus 12:14). God then emphasizes the importance of not changing the elements He provided for the meal, but always sticking with unleavened bread. "If anyone eats what is leavened, . . . that person shall be cut off from Israel" (Exodus 12:15). The Passover feast must never be taken for granted, but it must be celebrated faithfully, according to God's institution (vv. 14, 18). Obviously, Israel must regard this meal with the utmost seriousness, eating it in the manner it was given to them and not changing it according to their own desires.

Perhaps there is a parallel here between the Passover and the celebration of Holy Communion. Just as the Passover was to be a feast that was celebrated throughout many generations, so Jesus also commands, "Do this in remembrance of Me" (Luke 22:19). When God's people today celebrate Holy Communion, they also must celebrate it in the way Christ gave it to them. Jesus does not command that unleavened bread be used in the Lord's Supper, it is true. But He does give us bread and wine to use in this meal. Just as the people of the Old Testament were not permitted to substitute leavened bread for unleavened, so also ought Christians today not substitute other elements, such as grape juice or potato chips, for the bread and wine of Holy Communion. To do so would be to introduce uncertainty and doubt into God's sure and certain promises.

According to Exodus 12:17, what great event was the Passover meal created to help Israel remember? For how many years was this Passover to be celebrated? See also Deuteronomy 16:3.

God gave the Passover to enable His people to remember, commemorate, and participate in His great act of deliverance from the bondage of Egypt. This was a lasting ordinance, that is, a meal to be celebrated perpetually by God's people for generation after generation. Deuteronomy 16:3 shows that the people who celebrate the Passover—even many generations after the exodus—get incorporated through this meal into the exodus, even if they themselves were not originally part of it. These words in Deuteronomy 16 were not spoken to the people who originally left Egypt—they all died in the desert because of their rebellion against God (see Numbers 14:26–35 and Deuteronomy 1:3). Rather, these words were spoken to the next generation of Israelites, who were born during the forty years of wandering in the desert. They were not part of the exodus. Yet God does not say to this second generation, "Remember how I delivered your forefathers out of Egypt." He says instead, "remember the day when you came out of the land of Egypt" (Deuteronomy 16:3). By participating in the Passover meal, God's people became participants in salvation itself.

Many people might think that the Passover meal was only a symbol of God's salvation, or a memorial meal of how God saved Israel. How do Deuteronomy 16:2, 6 indicate that the Passover meal was more than a mere symbol or memorial?

While the people celebrated the Passover, they did so at the place "that the LORD will choose, to make His name dwell in there" (Deuteronomy 16:2, 6). Notice the verb God uses to describe His name: it *dwells* in the place of His choosing. Rocks do not dwell; dead bodies do not dwell; ideas do not dwell: only living things dwell. When God says that He will cause His name to dwell, He is talking about His living presence among His people. That is to say, when the people ate the Passover meal, they weren't simply eating a mere symbol of the exodus; they were participating in the eternal presence of the living God.

Hebrews 11:28 describes how Moses observed the Passover. What was the key to his keeping the feast rightly? In what did Moses place his faith, in the blood or in the promise attached to the blood?

Moses celebrated the Passover rightly because Moses lived by faith. He did not trust in the blood itself (recall Hebrews 10:4), but in the promise attached to the blood. God had said, "When I see the blood, I will pass over you, and no plague will befall you or destroy you, when I strike the land of Egypt" (Exodus 12:13). Moses observed the Passover by trusting not in the blood of the Passover lamb itself but in this great promise attached to the blood.

Compare what Martin Luther says about the Sacraments in his Large Catechism: "The Sacraments and all outward things that God ordains and institutes should not be considered according to the coarse, outward mask, the way we look at a nutshell. But we respect them because God's Word is included in them" (*Concordia,* LC IV 19).

Read Luke 22:1–23. Is there any significance in the fact that Jesus chose the Passover celebration as the time He would give His disciples the gift of Holy Communion?

By choosing the celebration of the Passover as the time to institute and give the gift of Holy Communion to His Church, Jesus opens the door for us to see great similarities between these two divinely given meals. Seminary professor Arthur Just comments,

> *Luke points to Jesus' death as the sacrificial Passover lamb who fulfills and renders obsolete the sacrifices of the OT [Old Testament]. This is the deeper and more important message of the narrative.* This *Feast of Unleavened Bread will be like none other. It falls on the day of Jesus' passion. The Passover lamb whose blood atones for all is Jesus, the Lamb of God, who takes away the sin of the world (John 1:29). The disciples prepared for this meal with expectations of celebrating another Jewish Passover with its fixed ritual of remembering God's gracious deliverance out of Egypt. But what the disciples experienced on this night in which Jesus was betrayed was not another Jewish Passover, but* Jesus' Passover, *in which he took the fixed ritual of the Passover Seder and gave everything in this meal new meaning. He gave it* Christological *meaning, as he interpreted the food at the meal, the story of the exodus, the broken bread and the cup of blessing* in terms of himself (Luke 9:51–24:53, *pp. 817–18).*

Conclusion

When Christians eat Christ's body and drink His blood in the meal of Holy Communion, they do not merely remember the events of His death or resurrection. Nor do they receive a simple representation of Christ's body and blood. Christians eat and drink of the *very* body and blood of Christ that was given for their forgiveness. They become participants in this great act of God's salvation, even though the crucifixion for sins took place many years ago. Just as the people of Israel participated in the exodus through their eating of the Passover, so also do God's people today participate in the crucifixion through the eating and drinking of Holy Communion.

Closing Prayer

Here the true Paschal Lamb we see,
Whom God so freely gave us;

He died on the accursed tree—
So strong His love—to save us.

See, His blood now marks our door;
Faith points to it; death passes o'er,

And Satan cannot harm us. Alleluia!

Then let us feast this Easter Day
On Christ, the bread of heaven;

The Word of grace has purged away
The old and evil leaven.

Christ alone our souls will feed;
He is our meat and drink indeed;

Faith lives upon no other! Alleluia!

Martin Luther, 1483–1546; tr. Richard Massie, 1800–87, alt.
(*LW* 123:3, 5)

Session 1

IN REMEMBRANCE OF ME

THE PASSOVER MEAL

Setting the Scene

Read **Genesis 41:53–42:5**. What first caused the family of Israel to visit Egypt? Who was already there, keeping charge of Egypt's grain storage? How is it that he ended up in such a powerful position? (To review the story, check **Genesis 37:26–28; 39; 41:25–45**.)

In **Genesis 50:19–21**, what explanation does Joseph give his brothers concerning God's purpose for Joseph's years of slavery and imprisonment? Who, then, ultimately saved the family of Israel by providing them with food? See **James 1:17**.

Where did Jacob (a.k.a. Israel) and his family eventually move, according to **Genesis 46:1–7**? In what way does this set the stage for the exodus, according to **Exodus 1:1–14**?

The Pharaoh refused to let God's people go, even after Egypt suffered nine horrible plagues. What tenth and final plague does God promise in **Exodus 11:4–8**? Who or what would be included in this plague, according to **verse 5**? In what way does this promise of destruction get fulfilled in **Exodus 12:29–32**?

Before we continue with this important Old Testament story, we need to be sure that we study it from New Testament perspective. What does Jesus say about the Old Testament in **John 5:39**? In **Luke 24:25–27**, what resource does the resurrected Jesus use to teach His disciples while traveling on the road to Emmaus? What insight does Peter add in **Acts 10:43**?

What image does St. Paul use to describe Jesus in **1 Corinthians 5:7**? How might this image influence the way you read **Exodus 12:1–28**, the story of the Passover?

A Special Meal

Read about God's gift of the Passover meal in **Exodus 12:1–28**. As you read, keep a list of things that remind you—even in a small way—of Jesus, His work of salvation for you, and how that work of salvation gets distributed to you today.

The first Passover meal involved a sacrificial lamb whose blood was shed to protect the people from judgment. What were the people instructed to do with the lamb in **Exodus 12:8**? In what way is this verse significant, not only for Old Testament believers, but also for Christians today?

What especially important characteristic must the Passover lamb have, according to **Exodus 12:5**? How does this compare to **1 Peter 1:18–19** and **Hebrews 4:15**?

What additional foods were to be eaten with the Passover lamb, according to **Exodus 12:8**? What significance might these foods have had for the people of Israel? See **Exodus 1:14** and **Deuteronomy 16:3**.

What promise does God speak to His people in **Exodus 12:7, 12–13**? What does the shedding of blood indicate, according to **Leviticus 17:11**? From what did the shed blood of the Passover lamb and the other Old Testament sacrifices ultimately offer God's people protection? See **Hebrews 9:22** and **1 John 1:7**.

Unleavened bread (that is, bread without yeast) symbolizes haste in the Passover meal. What meaning does Jesus attach to yeast in **Matthew 16:5–12**? How does St. Paul speak about yeast in **1 Corinthians 5:6–8**?

What help does **Hebrews 10:4** provide toward a right understanding of the Passover lamb and the other sacrifices of the Old Testament?

In what way might these words from Jesus and from St. Paul add significance to the unleavened bread, especially in light of **Exodus 12:19**?

Take a look at **Exodus 12:21–22**. What sort of "paintbrush" were the people to use for putting the blood of the Passover lamb on the doorposts of their houses? King David also speaks about this plant in **Psalm 51:7**. What might David have had in mind as he prayed for forgiveness of his sins?

God attaches a promise to His Passover meal (Exodus 12:13), but He also attaches a command to it. See **Exodus 12:14–20**. What did God command Israel concerning this meal? What punishments does He give for those who do not take the meal seriously and eat in a way that is contrary to the way God has commanded?

According to **Exodus 12:17**, what great event was the Passover meal created to help Israel remember? For how many years was this Passover to be celebrated? See also **Deuteronomy 16:3**.

Many people might think that the Passover meal was only a symbol of God's salvation, or a memorial meal of how God saved Israel. How does **Deuteronomy 16:2, 6** indicate that the Passover meal was more than a mere symbol or memorial?

Hebrews 11:28 describes how Moses observed the Passover. What was the key to his keeping the feast rightly? In what did Moses place his faith, in the blood or in the promise attached to the blood?

Read **Luke 22:1–23**. Is there any significance in the fact that Jesus chose the Passover celebration as the time He would give His disciples the gift of Holy Communion?

8

You Prepare a Table Before Me

The Wilderness Journey

Lesson Focus

"You open Your hand; You satisfy the desire of every living thing" (Psalm 145:16). God uses food not only to connect the nation of Israel from its exodus from Egyptian bondage but also to sustain them during their wilderness journey. This lesson will study the ways that God miraculously provided for His people Israel. In so doing, it will draw some parallels to the way God continues graciously to provide for His people even today.

Introduction

Discuss with the students a time when someone prepared a special dinner for them. Perhaps it was a birthday meal, a celebration of a sports victory, or "just because." When someone else goes to such elaborate lengths to make a meal for you, what message is that person speaking through his or her actions? How does that person feel about you?

The people of Israel, during their wilderness journey, had no way to provide for themselves. Yet God had not led them out to the middle of nowhere so they could starve! All through their journey, God lovingly and faithfully prepared a table for them (Psalm 23:5).

There are many parallels between the Israelites' journey through the wilderness and the everyday life of the Christian. Luther, as you will later see, referred to the Christian's daily living as a journey out of the "Egypt" of this difficult life to the "Promised Land" of eternal life in heaven. Yet, through all the difficulties of this journey, God promises faithfully to provide for our every need. The example of the Israelites in the wilderness shows that, even when we doubt and falter, our gracious Father in heaven does not fail.

Opening Prayer

Give us this day our daily bread. This bread is our Lord Jesus Christ who feeds and comforts the soul. Therefore, O heavenly Father, grant us grace that the life, word, works and sufferings of Christ may be preached, made known, and preserved for us and all the world. Help us to keep His words and works in all walks of life as a powerful example and an inducement to every virtue. Enable us in our sufferings and tribulations to be strengthened and comforted by His sufferings and cross. Help us to conquer our death by a firm faith in His victory over day and boldly follow our beloved Leader into the life beyond. Amen. (Luther's Prayers, *no. 55 pp. 25–26)*

Going Without

In Exodus 16:1–3, why might God have allowed the people to grow hungry before providing them with bread? In what way is hunger a great blessing from God? Take Psalm 145:15–16 into consideration.

God did not forget to provide for His people in the wilderness, but He deliberately allowed them to become hungry before providing them with food. In this way, He was able to focus their attention upon Him and to show them that He and He alone opens His hand and satisfies "the desire of every living thing" (Psalm 145:16).

It is necessary for God to treat His people this way because they quickly forget His benefits when things are going well for them. This is why the writer of Proverbs prays that God would not give him too much, "lest I be full and deny You and say, 'Who is the LORD?'" (30:9). Were they not so quick to forget His benefits, God would not need to allow His people to grow hungry and cry out to Him for food. But here He shows His grace and mercy, feeding His people in such a way as to continually remind them from whence their sustenance comes.

In what way does Jesus use hunger as a teaching tool in Matthew 5:6?

In His Sermon on the Mount, Jesus declares, "Blessed are those who hunger and thirst for righteousness, for they shall be satisfied" (Matthew 5:6). With these words, Jesus draws a parallel between physical hunger and spiritual hunger. Just as God "gives to the beast their food, and to the young ravens that cry" (Psalm 147:9), so also He provides righteousness to those who realize they have none and hunger for it. Professor David Scaer explains:

Hungering in the Fourth Beatitude [Matthew

5:6], "Blessed are those who hunger and thirst after righteousness, for they shall be satisfied," refers not to a physical hungering, but to an internal longing of the soul in its relationship to God. . . . The background is Israel's sojourning in the wilderness where for both food and water they were completely dependent upon God. The hungering and thirsting suggest that a person's total existence is dependent for life upon something outside of him. . . . In the Fourth Beatitude the blessed long for something which only God can satisfy. (The Sermon on the Mount, *pp. 84–85)*

These words suggest that hunger during Israel's travels in the wilderness meant more than merely filling peoples' bellies. Hunger—for ancient Israel and for God's people today—has to do with the realization that everything we possess, both physical and spiritual, comes from the gracious and generous hand of God.

When talking about the Lord's Supper in the Small Catechism, Luther mentioned hunger when he stated, "Fasting and bodily preparation are certainly fine outward training." In light of the previous question, what benefit might fasting provide for you as you prepare yourself to take Holy Communion?

Jesus' words in Matthew 5:6, above, show that fasting can be used as a good way of preparing for Holy Communion. As you feel the pangs of physical hunger, you can use these realizations as a way also of thinking about your spiritual hunger, which can only be satisfied by the gift of God's grace through Christ Jesus. When fasting is spoken about in the Scriptures, it commonly is related to sorrow over sin and repentance before God (e.g., see Joel 2:15–17 and Psalm 35:13). While Luther rejected fasts that were commanded by the Church, he also saw benefit in the Christian's voluntary abstention from food. Hunger helps the Christian avoid spiritual sloth:

It is right to fast frequently in order to subdue and control the body. For when the stomach is full, the body does not serve for preaching, for praying, for studying, or for doing anything else that is good. . . . But one should not fast with a view to meriting something by it as a good work. (What Luther Says, *no. 1514)*

For what miracle was God preparing the Israelites by allowing them to hunger, according to Exodus 16:4–8? What limitations did He place upon their gathering of food? Why were these limitations given?

By allowing Israel to hunger, God focused His people's attention on the miracle of the bread from heaven, which He promised to provide for them daily during their wilderness journey. God limited the people to gathering one day's portion for their families, with a two-day portion gathered on the day before the Sabbath. In this way, God intended to test their faith, "whether they will walk in My law or not" (Exodus 16:4).

Of course, God already knew whether or not the people would walk in His Law, that is, obey His commands. God knows all things before they even happen. God tested Israel in order to teach them faith. The test was for the peoples' benefit, not for God's. Some of the people ignored His Word and went their own way, collecting and hoarding the gifts that He gave to them (Exodus 16:20). They learned the hard way that it did not benefit them to ignore God and His Word. Other people gathered exactly as they had been commanded. In so doing, they saw the gracious hand of God continually open to them each day, providing for them according to their needs.

Give Us This Day . . .

In what way is Exodus 16:4 reflected in the Lord's Prayer? See Matthew 6:11 or Luke 11:3.

In the Lord's Prayer, God's children pray, "Give us this day our daily bread" (Matthew 6:11) or "Give us each day our daily bread" (Luke 11:3). As Israel waited patiently upon God for each day's care and provision, so Christians today rely upon God's gracious and daily care.

According to Luther's Small Catechism, what is meant by daily bread?

Luther includes an extensive list in his explanation to the Fourth Petition of the Lord's Prayer. Take a few minutes to think about and discuss how each of the things that Luther lists here relate to daily bread.

> *Daily bread includes everything that has to do with the support and needs of the body, such as food, drink, clothing, shoes, house, home, land, animals, money, goods, a devout husband or wife, devout children, devout workers, devout and faithful rulers, good government, good weather, peace, health, self-control, good reputation, good friends, faithful neighbors, and the like.* (SC, *pp. 18–19, 485)*

In Exodus 16:20 and 27–30, some of the Israelites were not content with God's gift of daily bread. What did they do? What happened as a result?

Discontent with God's daily provision tempted some of the Israelites to gather more manna than they needed for the day, hoarding God's gifts for themselves. Some people also went out to gather manna on the seventh day of the week, expressly ignoring the command that God had given to them through Moses, "Six days you shall gather it, but on the seventh day, which is a Sabbath, there will be none" (Exodus 16:26). As a result, both Moses (v. 20) and God (v. 28) became angry.

According to Matthew 6:25–34, what are you saying to God when you are content with your daily bread? What are you saying to Him when you feel the need to accumulate for yourself many possessions that go beyond your "daily bread"?

Contentment with daily bread expresses faith and trust in God, who provides you with all things. Just as the birds of the air and the flowers of the field do not allow themselves to worry about the care God has promised to give, so also can God's people contentedly rejoice that He provides for everything they need. When God's people worry and become anxious about what they shall eat and drink, they express doubt in God's willingness and/or His ability to provide. This is nothing other than a lack of faith. "But seek first the kingdom of God and His righteousness, and all these things will be added to you" (Matthew 6:33).

Of course, these gracious words from Jesus are not a license to laziness, as if Christians may simply lie down on the couch and expect God automatically to feed and clothe them! God provides for His people by means of their own labors or through the labors of others (as in the case of children, the elderly, or those who are otherwise unable to work). For this reason Paul warns, "If anyone is not willing to work, let him not eat" (2 Thessalonians 3:10).

> *The command not to be concerned about what shall be eaten and drunk complements the Fourth Beatitude: "Blessed are those who hunger and thirst for righteousness, for they shall be filled" ([Matthew] 5:6). The one desiring the higher food of God's righteousness revealed in Jesus can no longer be overly concerned or anxious about how he will be fed.* (The Sermon on the Mount, *p. 218)*

The reference to daily bread in the Lord's Prayer raises important questions for the way Christians manage their finances. For example, if you purchase a life insurance policy, are you expressing doubt that God will care for your loved ones after your death? If you carefully save money for college or for retirement, are you essentially saying to God that you are unsure He adequately will provide for these times in your life?

It would be unfair to make a generalization and say, "Retirement accounts, life insurance policies, and college savings all lack faith in God." Yes, God provides you with daily bread today, and your financial planning for the future could well be the way He provides for your daily bread tomorrow. Yet all such plans for the future must trust solely in God, and not in the plan itself. God must be loved and trusted more than the savings account or insurance policy (see Matthew 6:24). You might save thousands of dollars for college, but that savings could also suddenly disappear, if God sees fit. Your retirement account might be the way that God provides for you in old age, but He might choose a different way instead. The point of "daily bread" in the Lord's Prayer is not that Christians are forbidden to save for the future, but that the future belongs to God. Christians may live in the joy and contentment that

God shall indeed provide for them, not only today but all the days of their lives.

What name was given to this bread from heaven in Exodus 16:31? How long did God continue to provide this gift, according to Joshua 5:11–12? What provision did He make for Israel after that time?

"Now the house of Israel called its name manna" (Exodus 16:31). Scholars theorize that the name for this miraculous bread is derived from the Hebrew word for "what," as in, "What is this stuff?" See Exodus 16:15.

God miraculously provided this bread to Israel all during their many years in the wilderness. Joshua 5:12 explains, "The manna ceased the day after they ate of the produce of the land [of Canaan]. And there was no longer manna for the people of Israel, but they ate of the fruit of the land of Canaan that year."

> *The special detail in Joshua 5:11 about this particular unleavened bread [of the Passover celebration] is that it is made from the grain of the promised land and that it is eaten together with roasted grain. The Canaanites of the area evidently have fled their fields for the security of the gated and walled city of Jericho (Joshua 2:7, 15; 6:1). The Israelites are now eating from fields they did not plant, in fulfillment of God's promise in Deuteronomy 6:11.* (Joshua, *pp. 241–42)*

Realizing that the land of Canaan—the land God swore as a promise (Deuteronomy 34:4)—can be used as an image for our eternal home in heaven, what special comfort does Joshua 5:12 speak to God's children?

Comparing the daily life of the Church (and of individual Christians) to Israel's journey in the wilderness, Martin Luther observed that "we journey into the real promised land of heaven out of the real Egypt of this world" (*AE* 32:30).

Just as God faithfully provided for His people Israel all during their wilderness travel, so also Christians rejoice today that He will faithfully care for them during their travels through this "valley of sorrow" (Small Catechism, Seventh Petition) until they rest in heaven with Him. There may be times of great opulence and times of great need, but there will never be a time when God abandons His people. He shall remain with them, caring for their every need, until they enter the eternal land God promised to them in Christ.

In addition to the bread from heaven, what further miracle did God perform in Exodus 16:13? While this miracle may seem somewhat insignificant (especially because the rest of the chapter focuses exclusively on the bread), what importance does Numbers 11:31–33 attach to it?

When the people were dissatisfied with manna alone, God also provided them with quail to eat. The people again rebelled in Numbers 11, with some of "the rabble" (v. 4) craving the great variety of food that was available to them in Egypt. God sent another flock of quail, as He had done previously in Exodus 16:13. Even though it appeared that God had given in to the people's demands, this provision was not for the people's blessing, but for their judgment! The quail looked the same as before, but "while the meat was yet between their teeth, before it was consumed, the anger of the LORD was kindled against the people, and the LORD struck down the people with a very great plague. . . . There they buried the people who had the craving" (Numbers 11:33–34).

What important warning does Numbers 11 speak to all who eat the special food that God provides? Compare 1 Corinthians 11:27–30.

Paul warns the Corinthians, "Whoever, therefore, eats the bread or drinks the cup of the Lord in an unworthy manner will be guilty of profaning the body and blood of the Lord" (1 Corinthians 11:27). Just as the "rabble" (Numbers 11:4) among the Israelites failed to eat the manna in faith and thus received God's judgment, so also will all those be judged who profane the body and blood of the Lord by eating in an unworthy, faithless manner. "For anyone who eats and drinks without discerning the body eats and drinks judgment on himself" (1 Corinthians 11:29).

According to the Small Catechism, what makes you worthy to receive Holy Communion?

"That person is truly worthy and well prepared who has faith in these words, 'Given and shed for you for the forgiveness of sins.' But anyone who does not believe these words or doubts them is unworthy and unprepared, for the words 'for you' require all hearts to believe" (*SC,* pp. 29, 238). The faith to trust this promise is the free gift of our gracious God.

When the people saw God speaking His Ten Commandments to Moses on Mount Sinai, what did they do (Exodus 20:18–21)? Why did they do this? Compare Isaiah 6:1–5.

The people saw God's greatness and power expressed in flashes of thunder and lightning, smoke and trumpet blasts. This caused them to tremble with fear and beg of Moses, "You speak to us, and we will listen; but do not let God speak to us, lest we die" (Exodus 20:19).

When the prophet Isaiah had a similar experience, recorded in Isaiah 6, he despaired. "Woe is me! For I am lost; for I am a man of unclean lips, and I dwell in the midst of a people of unclean lips; for my eyes have seen the King, the LORD of hosts!" (Isaiah 6:5). Surely this same sort of fear gripped the Israelites at Mount Sinai! They had grumbled against God (that is, they had "unclean lips") and now God revealed His powerful presence to them. The realization of His great holiness, coupled with the realization of their sin, caused them their fear. Had they no sin, they would have had no reason to fear.

Later, in Exodus 24:9–11, many people climbed Mount Sinai. Who were they? Whom did they represent?

Seventy elders climbed Mount Sinai with Moses in order to enter into God's presence. These elders appear to have been in charge of representing each of the tribes of Israel in God's presence. The nation was too large for Moses to speak to all together, so he would speak to the elders instead. They, in turn, would go and speak to the people over whom they were given authority (see Exodus 3:15–18; 12:21–22; 17:5–6).

Since it was impossible for the entire nation to climb the mountain, these seventy elders represented the people in the presence of God. Like the rest of the people, the elders greatly feared God's presence. However, when "they saw the God of Israel . . . He did not lay His hand on the chief men of the people of Israel" (Exodus 24:10–11).

In Exodus 24:4–8, what act calmed the fears these men felt about the presence of God?

Moses offered burnt offerings and peace offerings to the LORD (Exodus 24:5). After he read God's Word to the people, "Moses took the blood and threw it on the people and said, 'Behold the blood of the covenant that the LORD has made with you in accordance with all these words'" (Exodus 24:8). The shed blood of the sacrificial victim thus covered the people and their sins, so that they could safely stand in the holy presence of God. This event may have come to John's mind when he wrote concerning Jesus, "the blood of Jesus His [God's] Son cleanses us from all sin" (1 John 1:7).

What similarity do you see between Moses' words in Exodus 24:8 and Jesus' words in Matthew 26:26–28?

Echoing Moses' words to Israel, Jesus gave His disciples the cup of Holy Communion and said to them, "This is My blood of the covenant" (v. 28). Just as the sacrificial bull shed his blood to cover the people and join them to the great promises of God, so it is with Jesus Himself. Having shed His blood for our salvation, Jesus now connects us to His covenant by giving us His own blood. Where Moses threw the blood, Jesus joins it to wine, that it may be drunk by His followers.

When translating Jesus' words of institution from Greek to English, some people prefer to use the word *testament* instead of *covenant.* This translation is helpful in that it emphasizes the "last will and testament" nature of Holy Communion. Christ Himself gave this gift to the Church and no one ought to change or alter its use (e.g., by substituting grape juice for wine, or by teaching that Jesus meant "this *represents* My body . . . blood" rather than "this *is* My body . . . blood"). Just as no court of law would ever allow you to change your relative's last will and testament, especially after that person died, so also must Christians keep Christ's last will and testament faithfully, in keeping with the way He gave it.

However, there is a cost to translating the word *covenant* as *testament.* As seminary professor David Scaer observes,

> *"Testament" in place of "covenant" only mutes the rich Old Testament history embedded in the Hebrew word b'rith, a concept that Matthew brings into the Eucharist. God's special relationship with Israel was established through a succession of covenants that culminated in the covenant at Sinai, in which Israel was confirmed as God's people (Exodus 24).*
>
> *In setting forth the Eucharist as a perpetual meal that commemorates the covenant Jesus made between God and the church, Matthew has in mind one particular covenant that God established with Israel through Moses. The parallels between Exodus 24 and Matthew's account of the institution of the Eucharist are arresting. In the first covenant, young men are commanded to offer burnt offerings and peace offerings by sacrificing young bulls. After the blood of the sacrificed animals is poured into basins, half is thrown on the altar and the other half is sprinkled by Moses on the people with the words: "Behold the blood of the covenant" (Exodus 24:8). These words certainly lie behind the words of Jesus: "This is my blood of the covenant" ([Matthew] 26:28).* (Discourses in Matthew, *p. 198)*

Conclusion

The people of Israel were joined to the covenant through the shedding of blood, having heard the Word of the Lord read by God's prophet, Moses. The whole event reaches culmination when the seventy elders—representing the entire people of Israel—"went up, and they saw the God of Israel. . . . They beheld God, and ate and drank" (Exodus 24:9–11).

Isn't this very similar to what every Christian is allowed to do at Holy Communion? Here, where the body and blood of Christ are joined to bread and wine, we through faith behold God. He is present in the cup; He is present in the bread; we eat and drink in His presence, having been fully cleansed of all our sins by the blood of the last sacrifice, Jesus Christ, our Lord.

Closing Prayer

O living Bread from heaven,
How well You feed Your guest!
The gifts that You have given
Have filled my heart with rest.
Oh, wondrous food of blessing,
Oh, cup that heals our woes!
My heart, this gift possessing,
With praises overflows. Amen.

Johann Rist, 1606–67; tr. Catherine Winkworth,1829–78, alt.
(*LW* 244:1)

You Prepare a Table before Me

The Wilderness Journey

Going Without

In **Exodus 16:1–3**, why might God have allowed the people to grow hungry before providing them with bread? In what way is hunger a great blessing from God? Take **Psalm 145:15–16** into consideration.

For what miracle was God preparing the Israelites by allowing them to hunger, according to **Exodus 16:4–8**? What limitations did He place upon their gathering of food? Why were these limitations given?

In what way does Jesus use hunger as a teaching tool in **Matthew 5:6**?

When talking about the Lord's Supper in the Small Catechism, Luther mentioned hunger when he stated, "Fasting and bodily preparation are certainly fine outward training." In light of the previous question, what benefit might fasting provide for you as you prepare yourself to take Holy Communion?

Give Us This Day . . .

In what way is **Exodus 16:4** reflected in the Lord's Prayer? See **Matthew 6:11** or **Luke 11:3**.

According to Luther's Small Catechism, what is meant by daily bread?

In **Exodus 16:20** and **27–30**, some of the Israelites were not content with God's gift of daily bread. What did they do? What happened as a result?

According to **Matthew 6:25–34**, what are you saying to God when you are content with your daily bread? What are you saying to Him when you feel the need to accumulate for yourself many possessions that go beyond your "daily bread"?

The reference to daily bread in the Lord's Prayer raises important questions for the way Christians manage their finances. For example, if you purchase a life insurance policy, are you expressing doubt that God will care for your loved ones after your death? If you carefully save money for college or for retirement, are you essentially saying to God that you are unsure He adequately will provide for these times in your life?

What name was given to this bread from heaven in **Exodus 16:31**? How long did God continue to provide this gift, according to **Joshua 5:11–12**? What provision did He make for Israel after that time?

Realizing that the land of Canaan—the land God swore as a promise—can be used as an image for our eternal home in heaven, what special comfort does **Joshua 5:12** speak to God's children?

In addition to the bread from heaven, what further miracle did God perform in **Exodus 16:13**? While this miracle may seem somewhat insignificant (especially because the rest of the chapter focuses exclusively on the bread), what importance does **Numbers 11:31–33** attach to it?

What important warning does **Numbers 11** speak to all who eat the special food that God provides? Compare **1 Corinthians 11:27–30**.

According to the Small Catechism, what makes you worthy to receive Holy Communion?

When the people saw God speaking His Ten Commandments to Moses on Mount Sinai, what did they do (**Exodus 20:18–21**)? Why did they do this? Compare **Isaiah 6:1–5**.

Later, in **Exodus 24:9–11**, many people climbed Mount Sinai. Who were they? Whom did they represent?

In **Exodus 24:4–8**, what act calmed the fears these men felt about the presence of God?

What similarity do you see between Moses' words in **Exodus 24:8** and Jesus' words in **Matthew 26:26–28**?

3

IN THE PRESENCE OF MY ENEMIES

DAVID AND DANIEL

Lesson Focus

"You open Your hand; You satisfy the desire of every living thing" (Psalm 145:16). God uses food not only to save the nation of Israel as a whole but also to save individuals. This lesson will study the examples of two prominent Old Testament men, both of whom received God's special care and provision by means of food. King David ate the food set aside especially for the priests; the prophet Daniel and his friends grew strong on food eaten by faith.

Introduction

Careful study of the examples of David (in 1 Samuel 21:1–9) and Daniel (Daniel 1:1–16) will lead the students into a deeper understanding of the blessings and benefits offered to Christians today in Holy Communion. It is not that either David or Daniel celebrated the Lord's Supper! However, God graciously dealt with each of these men by means of food. In so doing, He preserved their lives, even in the presence of their enemies.

David's enemy was King Saul, from whom he was running when he came to the tabernacle at the town of Nob. Tired and hungry, David asked the priest for something to eat. The priest gave the only bread that was available—the special bread of the Presence that only the priests were to eat. David ate the bread by faith and, in so doing, his life was preserved. In the same way, the "royal priesthood" (1 Peter 2:9)—which is another name for Christians —likewise eats a meal that is specially set apart for them. In so doing, their lives are preserved against all their enemies, which Martin Luther identified in his explanation of the Sixth Petition of the Lord's Prayer as "the devil, the world, and our sinful nature" (*SC*, pp. 19, 190–91).

Daniel's enemy was King Nebuchadnezzar, who had destroyed Jerusalem and taken captive all of the best young men of Israel. Rather than living by the rules and customs of idolatrous Babylon, Daniel and his three friends refused to accept the rich and sumptuous food the king required them to eat. Living by faith and trusting in God, they chose instead a simple meal that outwardly did not seem fit to nourish them. However, God protected Daniel and his friends through this simple food. In the same way, God provides for His Christians even today, nourishing and protecting them through the simple food of Holy Communion.

Opening Prayer

The eyes of all look to You, and You give them their food in due season. You open Your hand; You satisfy the desire of every living thing. The LORD is righteous in all His ways and kind in all His works. The LORD is near to all who call on Him, to all who call on Him in truth. He fulfills the desire of those who fear Him; He also hears their cry and saves them. (Psalm 145:15–19)

Food on the Run

What sort of furniture did God command His people to build in Exodus 25:23–30? What special purpose was this furniture to serve, according to verse 30?

God commanded that the people build a special table, overlaid with pure gold, for the purpose of holding the "bread of the Presence" (Exodus 25:30). God said that this table must stand in His presence, that is, in the tabernacle sanctuary (and later, in the temple).

It is interesting to note that God choose acacia wood for this table, not olive or cedar, or some other wood that is found in the Middle East. The acacia tree is large and good for high-quality timber, but its true significance is that its resin preserves it against rot, a fact even noted by Martin Luther (*AE* 17:49). Elsewhere, Luther described the wood as "incorruptible" (AE 29:201). The table for the bread of the Presence was possibly made of acacia (as was the ark of the covenant; see Exodus 25:10) partly to further emphasize the permanent, abiding presence of God among His people.

Leviticus 24:5–9 describes how the bread of the Presence was to be made and used. How many loaves were there? What do you think these loaves represented?

The bread of the Presence consisted of twelve loaves in all, each one representing a tribe of Israel. Usually, when the number twelve appears in the Old

Testament, it refers to God's people. See, for example, the twelve pillars of the Sinai altar (Exodus 24:4), the twelve stones of the high priest's ephod (Exodus 28:21), the twelve oxen offered to the Lord for use in transporting the tabernacle (Numbers 7:3), and Joshua's pillar of twelve stones that commemorated Israel's entry into Canaan (Joshua 4:9).

Notice also that these loaves were sprinkled with frankincense, a powder made from the resin of a balsam tree that was burned during prayer. David wrote, "Let my prayer be counted as incense before You" (Psalm 141:2). When John wrote the Book of Revelation, he described "golden bowls full of incense, which are the prayers of the saints" (Revelation 5:8). Realizing the close relationship between incense and prayer, perhaps we may conclude that the bread of the Presence did not merely represent God's people in a general sense, but rather, this bread specifically represented God's repentant and prayerful people who wait in His presence.

According to Exodus 25:8, whose presence does this bread indicate? Compare also Exodus 33:14–15 and Isaiah 63:9.

The bread of the Presence indicated that the Lord was continually present with and among His people. In Exodus 33:14–15, God promises Moses, "My presence will go with you." Isaiah spoke about "the angel of His presence" (Isaiah 63:9), which quite likely speaks about God the Son.

Each Sabbath, Aaron (and his successors) would carefully arrange these twelve loaves of bread into two piles in the presence of the Lord as a food offering to the Lord on behalf of the people. Just as these loaves of bread rested continually in the safety and protection of the tabernacle (in the Lord's presence), so also God's people enjoy His watchful care and protection throughout their lives.

Returning to Leviticus 24:5–9, who was allowed to eat the bread of the Presence? According to verse 7, was this bread particularly tasty? Why would this bread have been desirable to eat? See verse 9.

According to the Lord's command, only Aaron and his sons, along with all the priests who came after them, were allowed to eat the bread of the Presence. Having been seasoned with frankincense, this bread probably did not taste especially good. (Try chewing some dried pine pitch to get an idea of the flavor.) Yet this bread was not eaten because of its "food value" or its taste. Aaron and his sons ate the bread in faith, because the Lord commanded it, and because the Lord regarded it as "a most holy portion" (v. 9).

What points of comparison between the bread of the Presence and the meal of Holy Communion do these questions and answers provide you with?

When God gives a command—even one that sounds strange, like eating incense-covered bread—He always attaches a great blessing to the command. "Blessed . . . are those who hear the word of God and keep it" (Luke 11:28). Yet the blessing and benefit might not always be immediately apparent. Aaron and his sons must eat by faith.

In the same way, just as Aaron and his sons ate bread at God's command, and ate by faith in God's Word and promise, so also do Christians today eat and drink at God's command when they participate in Holy Communion. In so doing, they receive the unseen benefits of "forgiveness of sins, life, and salvation" (*SC,* pp. 29, 233).

Read about King David in 1 Samuel 21:1–9. Whom did he visit? How did this fellow feel about David's arrival? Compare 1 Samuel 21:7 with 22:17–18 to discover a possible reason for this man's reaction.

"David came to Nob to Ahimelech the priest" (1 Samuel 21:1). The tabernacle had been set up at Nob, and Ahimelech was the priest in charge of its care. But rather than joyously welcoming God's specially chose king, "Ahimelech came to meet David trembling" (1 Samuel 21:1). Exhausted from his journey, David asked Ahimelech for some bread to eat.

Troublesome times had fallen upon David. King Saul had become so jealous of the new king that he wanted to kill David. David had run away from Saul, coming to Nob. When he arrived, he discovered that

Doeg the Edomite, Saul's chief herdsman, was also at the tabernacle. David did not feel threatened by this, but Ahimelech's trembling suggests that the priest feared the consequences David's arrival. Doeg the Edomite later proved to be David's enemy, obeying Saul's command to kill all the priests, even when the king's guards refused to do so. That day, Doeg the Edomite killed eighty-five priests (including Ahimelech) and the entire population of the town, along with all its livestock (1 Samuel 22:18–19). This carnage suggests the deep resentment and jealousy that Saul felt for David, which was so great that even children and infants suffered his wrath.

What special food did Ahimelech give to David? Bearing in mind Leviticus 24:5–9, ought David to have eaten this bread?

David asked for five loaves of ordinary bread. Having none, Ahimelech offered him the consecrated bread of the Presence, which the priests still laid out before the Lord every Sabbath. Because the bread of the Presence was to be eaten by the priests only, David ought not to have given it to his men or eaten it himself. On the surface, both Ahimelech and David broke the Levitical law.

Think about how this event might be reflected in the words David wrote in Psalm 23:5.

In Psalm 23:5, David rejoiced that God prepares "a table before me in the presence of my enemies." Here at Nob, David eats the bread of the Presence in the presence of his enemies: Doeg the Edomite is already there at the tabernacle, and King Saul is pursuing David closely. Yet David eats without fear. God has provided nourishment and strength for the cross David must bear.

What use does Jesus later make of David's actions in Matthew 12:1–8?

One day, while Jesus and His disciples were passing through some grain fields, His disciples began to pick the heads of wheat, roll them between their hands to remove the chaff, and eat them. This would not have been a problem, except that it was the Sabbath. When the Pharisees challenged Jesus for allowing His disciples to "break" the Sabbath laws in this manner, Jesus immediately pointed them to David's eating of the bread of the Presence at Nob. "Have you not read what David did when he was hungry, and those who were with him: how he entered the house of God and ate the bread of the Presence, which it was not lawful for him to eat nor for those who were with him, but only for the priests?" (Matthew 12:3–4).

Jesus is *not* suggesting that two wrongs make a right! He is not claiming that, since David broke the Sabbath, He and His disciples can also. Rather, Jesus points to David as an example of one who rightly understood the sacrificial laws of the Old Testament. David knew that God does not care only about the sacrifices themselves—whether the blood sacrifices or the food sacrifices, such as the bread of the Presence. God cares about mercy and about showing mercy to those who need it. Ahimelech acted rightly by giving David the bread of the Presence, and David acted rightly by eating it, because God desires "mercy, and not sacrifice" (Matthew 12:7).

What did Jesus—and David—understand about the bread of the Presence that the Pharisees failed to grasp? Which is more important to our heavenly Father, His things or His people?

Of course, God loves His people more than anything else in all creation. In fact, He loves us so much that He even sacrificed His Son for us and for our salvation! Jesus and David both knew that the bread of the Presence was not placed before God for God's sake, but it was there for the sake of God's people. This bread was an everlasting indicator that God would always and faithfully remain with His people. It was *not* an indicator that His people would always remain faithful to Him (Old Testament history repeatedly shows how impossible it was for the people to remain faithful for very long).

When we realize that the bread of the Presence was placed in the sanctuary for the sake of God's people and not for God's sake, David's actions make more sense. He was needy when he came to God's presence. God graciously met his need. This is the sort of thing that God rejoices to do for His people.

This passage points toward the true nature of Christian worship—worship does not focus primarily on our service to God—but on God's service to us. Just as David received nourishment and refreshment from God by eating the bread of the Presence, so also God's people receive good gifts from Him in worship.

If only the priests were allowed to eat the bread of the Presence (recall Leviticus 24:5–9), what does it say about David that God allowed him to eat this bread?

It does not seem unfair to conclude that God regarded David as a priest. Since the priests were the only ones allowed to eat the bread, and since David ate it without any punishment, it appears that God regarded David as one of His priests, even though David was not from the tribe of Levi.

In a similar way, how do 1 Peter 2:9 and Revelation 1:6 describe you and all Christians? What special bread has God given you that you may eat without fear of judgment in the same way that David ate?

In his first epistle, Peter reminds us that all Christians are priests: "You are a chosen race, a royal priesthood, a holy nation, a people for His [God's] own possession, that you may proclaim the excellencies of Him who called you out of darkness into His marvelous light" (1 Peter 2:9).

> *The apostle gives the Christians a proper title. He took this statement from Moses, who tells the Jews in Deuteronomy. 7:6: "You are a people holy to the Lord your God; the Lord your God has chosen you to be a people for His own possession, out of all the peoples that are on the face of the earth." And in Exodus 19:5–6 we read: "You shall be My own possession among all peoples . . . and you shall be to Me a kingdom of priests and a holy nation" (AE 30:62).*

Revelation 1:6 adds that Jesus, by His death and resurrection for our sins, has made us "priests to His God and Father." This means that, because the blood of Christ has washed away all our sins, we may now stand in God's presence without fear. As David piously and fearlessly ate the bread of the Presence, which was intended only for priests, so also may God's people eat the bread (and wine) of Holy Communion. Because He has made us His priests, we may eat of this sacred meal in the same way that David ate—piously and without fear.

Picky Eaters

Read about another food miracle in Daniel 1:1–16. According to this account, what sort of food did King Nebuchadnezzar give the captive Israelites to eat (v. 5)? Did Daniel and his friends eat this food? Why or why not? See especially verse 8.

After King Nebuchadnezzar and the armies of Babylon destroyed Jerusalem, he brought many of the best and brightest young men of Israel into captivity. Among them were Daniel and his three friends, Hananiah, Mishael, and Azariah (a.k.a. Shadrach, Meshach, and Abednego). Nebuchadnezzar planned to train these men in the arts and sciences of Babylon, so that they might serve him in his royal court.

Nebuchadnezzar spared no expense in caring for the Israelite captives. "The king assigned them a daily portion of the food that the king ate, and of the wine that he drank" (Daniel 1:5). This sumptuous food was intended not only to nourish and strengthen the captives, but also to capture their hearts and minds. Why would the young men ever want to return to the smoldering ashes of Jerusalem and to the destroyed croplands of Israel when they could spend the rest of their lives enjoying the rich foods of the Babylonian court?

Daniel—along with his three friends—"resolved that he would not defile himself with the king's food, or with the wine that he drank" (Daniel 1:8). It is likely that the Israelites considered these foods contaminated and unholy because they had been previously sacrificed to idols.

What food did Daniel and his friends choose to eat instead? Struggling with his sense of reason, what did the jailer think about this idea (v. 10)?

Rather than disobey the ceremonial laws that God had given, Daniel and his friends chose instead to limit their diet to vegetables and water. Of course, the jailer objected because he was given responsibility for Daniel and his friends. If their health failed, he would die! "I fear my lord the king, who assigned your food and your drink; for why should he see that you were in worse condition than the youths who are of your own age? So you would endanger my head with the king" (Daniel 1:10).

Did Daniel rely on reason? On what did he rely? What promise did Daniel make to the jailer in verses 12–13? Was this self-confidence on Daniel's part?

By comparison to the jailer, Daniel and his friends relied not on reason, but on faith. More to the point, Daniel and his friends ate by faith, believing that the seemingly unbeneficial food would sustain and strengthen them. Confident that the Lord would watch over them, Daniel promised the jailer, "Test your servants for ten days; let us be given vegetables to eat and water to drink. Then let our appearance and the appearance of the youths who eat the king's food be observed by you, and deal with your servants according to what you see" (Daniel 1:12–13).

Daniel was certainly not speaking out of self-confidence. Nor did he trust in the "food value" of the vegetables and water. Daniel spoke God's prophetic Word, for he was a prophet (Matthew 24:15). He did not dream up this plan for himself, but he spoke with confidence in the Word and promise of God.

What change did the jailer see in Daniel and his friends after ten days? Was it the food that caused this improvement, or something else?

The jailer expected to see Daniel and his friends languishing because of their poor diet. Miraculously, "at the end of ten days it was seen that they were better in appearance and fatter in flesh than all the youths who ate the king's food" (Daniel 1:15). It was not the food itself that provided so wondrously for Daniel and his friends! God's promise was attached to the food.

Holy Communion can be compared to Daniel's diet: both are comprised of simple elements, but neither outwardly appears to be sufficient for healthy living. In what way does Daniel's example help you understand more deeply the blessing and benefit of Holy Communion?

Even though communicants receive only a tiny morsel of bread and a sip of wine, God's Word and promise are attached to this meal. In Holy Communion, Christians are nourished with "forgiveness of sins, life, and salvation" (*SC,* pp. 29, 233). But this nourishment does not come from the "food value" of the bread and the wine! These outward elements merely convey to you the Word and promise of God—and they give you health and life—just as the seemingly poor fare of vegetables and water provided for Daniel and his friends.

Recall Martin Luther's question and answer in the Small Catechism:

> How can bodily eating and drinking do such great things?
>
> *Certainly not just eating and drinking do these things, but the words written here: "Given and shed for you for the forgiveness of sins." These words, along with the bodily eating and drinking, are the main thing in the Sacrament. Whoever believes these words has exactly what they say: "forgiveness of sins."* (SC, *pp. 29, 236)*

Just as the seemingly insignificant vegetables and water did miraculous things for Daniel and his friends, so also do the plain and simple elements of bread and wine, body and blood, in Holy Communion do miraculous things for you!

Conclusion

Faith rests entirely on the Word and promise of God. When Jesus says, "Take, eat," you may approach the Lord's Supper with the same confidence by which David took from the sacred bread of the Presence and ate it. You may do this because God's Word declares that you—like David—are a "royal priesthood" (1 Peter 2:9). When Jesus says in Holy Communion, "Given and shed for you," you may eat this simple meal with Daniel's confidence, knowing that it is not the bread and wine that nourishes you (any more than vegetables and water nourished Daniel), but that this is the Lord's meal, given to you for your health and life.

Closing Prayer

Give thanks to the LORD, for He is good. His love endures forever.

[He] gives food to every creature. His love endures forever.

He provides food for the cattle and for the young ravens when they call. His pleasure is not in the strength of the horse, nor His delight in the legs of a man; the LORD delights in those who fear Him, who put their hope in His unfailing love. (Psalm 136:1, 25; 147:9–11 NIV)

We thank You, Lord God, heavenly Father, for all Your benefits, through Jesus Christ, our Lord, who lives and reigns with You and the Holy Spirit forever and ever. Amen. (*SC*, p. 32)

In the Presence of My Enemies

David and Daniel

Food on the Run

What sort of furniture did God command His people to build in **Exodus 25:23–30**? What special purpose was this furniture to serve, according to **verse 30**?

Leviticus 24:5–9 describes how the bread of the Presence was to be made and used. How many loaves were there? What do you think these loaves represented?

According to **Exodus 25:8**, whose presence does this bread indicate? Compare also **Exodus 33:14–15** and **Isaiah 63:9**.

Returning to **Leviticus 24:5–9**, who was allowed to eat the bread of the Presence? According to **verse 7**, was this bread particularly tasty? Why would this bread have been desirable to eat? See **verse 9.**

What points of comparison between the bread of the Presence and the meal of Holy Communion do these questions and answers provide you with?

Read about King David in **1 Samuel 21:1–9**. Whom did he visit? How did this fellow feel about David's arrival? Compare **1 Samuel 21:7** with **22:17–18** to discover a possible reason for this man's reaction.

What special food did Ahimelech give to David? Bearing in mind **Leviticus 24:5–9**, ought David to have eaten this bread?

Think about how this event might be reflected in the words David wrote in **Psalm 23:5**.

What use does Jesus later make of David's actions in **Matthew 12:1–8**?

What did Jesus—and David—understand about the bread of the Presence that the Pharisees failed to grasp? Which is more important to our heavenly Father, His things or His people?

If only the priests were allowed to eat the bread of the Presence (recall **Leviticus 24:5–9**), what does it say about David that God allowed him to eat this bread?

In a similar way, how do **1 Peter 2:9** and **Revelation 1:6** describe you and all Christians? What special bread has God given you that you may eat without fear of judgment in the same way that David ate?

Picky Eaters

Read about another food miracle in **Daniel 1:1–16**. According to this account, what sort of food did King Nebuchadnezzar give the captive Israelites to eat (**v. 5**)? Did Daniel and his friends eat this food? Why or why not? See especially **verse 8**.

What food did Daniel and his friends choose to eat instead? Struggling with his sense of reason, what did the jailer think about this idea (**v. 10**)?

Did Daniel rely on reason? On what did he rely? What promise did Daniel make to the jailer in **verses 12–13**? Was this self-confidence on Daniel's part?

What change did the jailer see in Daniel and his friends after ten days? Was it the food that caused this improvement, or something else?

Holy Communion can be compared to Daniel's diet: both are comprised of simple elements, but neither outwardly appears to be sufficient for healthy living. In what way does Daniel's example help you understand more deeply the blessing and benefit of Holy Communion?

4

My Cup Overflows

Elijah and the Widow

Lesson Focus

"My cup overflows" (Psalm 23:5). This lesson will take a look at the prophet Elijah, and how God miraculously provided food for His servant not once, but twice. God likewise promises to provide for His people even today. Christians may at various times experience both plenty and need. Some Christians may have more possessions and riches in this life than others do. Elijah's example shows that, whether we are rich or poor, all good things come from God. When Christians realize this, they are able rightly to receive their gifts of daily bread with thanksgiving.

Introduction

Have you ever needed to say something that you knew would get you into trouble? Perhaps it was a political conversation in which most of the people were expressing views different from your own. Or maybe it was something as simple as rooting for your favorite sports team, the perennial underdogs. How does it feel to say things that nobody else wants to hear? Which would you rather do—speak honestly and take the heat, or just keep your mouth shut and pretend your message doesn't matter?

Elijah's faithful proclamation of the Word landed him in trouble. While it certainly might have been easier for him to ignore the faithful preaching of the Word in order to remain in King Ahab's good graces, Elijah feared God more than men (Matthew 10:28; Acts 5:29).

Yet Elijah's fear of God was not a cringing fear that acts in order to escape punishment. Elijah's fear was the fear of faith. On the one hand, he knew that he must preach faithfully because God required it. On the other, he trusted that God is more than able to get His servant out of any trouble that faithful preaching might create for him. Just as Abraham before him realized, when offering Isaac as a sacrifice (Genesis 22), that God is able to raise the dead (Hebrews 11:17–19), so also Elijah realized that God is more than able to provide food even in the midst of horrible famine and drought. What God promises, God shall fulfill—even with a tiny, half-empty jug of oil and a small handful of flour!

Opening Prayer

Dear God, why should I be anxious and worry about my body and its food? How do You raise up the grain on the field and all the fruits? The world with all its wisdom and power is not able to make a stalk, a tiny leaf, or a flower. In You I have a Lord who can multiply one loaf as much as He pleases, without the aid of a farmer, a miller, or a baker. As you do this day by day, why should I worry whether You can or will supply my bodily needs? (Luther's Prayers, *no. 206, p. 100)*

Bird Food

What sermon did Elijah preach to King Ahab in 1 Kings 17:1?

Elijah, God's chosen prophet, went to King Ahab and preached that there would be a severe drought (and with it, famine) in the land. "There shall be neither dew nor rain these years, except by my word" (1 Kings 17:1). This drought lasted at least three years (1 Kings 18:1).

According to 1 Kings 16:29–34, what evil had Ahab done? Who else was included in the drought God visited on Ahab?

God used Elijah to proclaim the drought as a call to repentance for Ahab because Ahab "did evil in the sight of the LORD, more than all [the other kings] who were before him" (1 Kings 16:30). Ahab committed repeated acts of idolatry, not only following the notorious example of evil king Jeroboam (see 1 Kings 13:33–34; 14:6–11), but also taking a treacherous and idolatrous woman named Jezebel as his wife. "Ahab did more to provoke the LORD, the God of Israel, to anger than all the kings of Israel who were before him" (1 Kings 16:33).

Although Ahab is specifically named as having committed these idolatrous acts, the entire nation of Israel is called to repentance through the coming drought and famine. Everybody gets hungry during such horrible times! While 1 Kings 16 and 17 do not expressly state that the Israelites followed after Ahab's evil example, Old Testament history repeatedly suggests that the people were always quick to fall away from the Lord and to commit acts of idolatry (recall, for example, the worship of the golden calf in Exodus 32). It would not be difficult to imagine that many Israelites participated in Ahab's idolatry.

Even if the people did not follow Ahab's evil ways, there is still a sense in which all of God's people are in this situation together, whether or not they commit the idolatrous acts themselves. The example of Achan, son of Carmi, is instructive (see Joshua 7). God had commanded that, when the Israelites attacked Jericho, no one could keep any of the spoils of war. Rather, "the city and all that is within it shall be devoted to the LORD for destruction" (Joshua 6:17). But Achan simply could not allow all of that beautiful loot to be destroyed. He "took some of the devoted things. And the anger of the LORD burned against the people of Israel" (Joshua 7:1).

This is the point—God's anger burned against the whole nation, even though only one man sinned. All the people become involved in Achan's theft, in which he rejected the Word and command of God. This is why the army of Israel was beaten so badly in the battle of Ai (Joshua 7:1–5). Likewise, the entire nation suffered during the famine caused by Ahab's idolatrous acts.

It would be worthy discussion to consider the possibility that God's people today might also suffer some sort of evil or misfortune because of unrepentant acts of sin in their midst, even if they themselves do not indulge in the sin. For example, the sin of divorce brings suffering not only to husband and wife, but also to their children, their parents, their friends, and their fellow Christians. These other people may not have committed the act of divorce themselves. In most cases they bear no responsibility for the sin, but they are nevertheless implicated in its consequences. Might the same also be true of such "churchly" sins as advocating woman's ordination, the act of cohabitation before marriage, and church members who never bother to come to worship? What might be the larger, congregational consequences of such seemingly individual sins?

God then gave Elijah special instructions in 1 Kings 17:2–4. What command does God speak? What promise did He attach to His command?

In order to protect His dear prophet, God commanded Elijah to "depart from here and turn eastward and hide yourself by the brook Cherith, which is east of the Jordan" (1 Kings 17:3–4). Yet God does not send His servant away empty. Rather, He attaches a great promise to His command, which Elijah will depend upon for his very life: "You shall drink from the brook, and I have commanded the ravens to feed you there" (1 Kings 17:4). Ever faithful to every promise, God sent the ravens, who brought Elijah "bread and meat in the morning, and bread and meat in the evening" (1 Kings 17:6).

In what way might this "promise attached to a command" that God spoke to Elijah help us to understand Jesus' commands in Matthew 26:26–28?

At the Last Supper, Jesus commanded His disciples, "Take, eat; . . . drink of it" (Matthew 26:26–27). Since Jesus gives Holy Communion in the form of a command, many people wrongly conclude that this meal is an act that we do for God. However, by focusing on their own action, they ignore the promise attached to the command, namely, "this is . . . for the forgiveness of sins" (Matthew 26:28).

Think about Holy Communion in light of the "promise attached to a command" that God spoke to Elijah. God did not send Elijah to the Cherith brook because He wanted to see if Elijah was able to obey, or in order to test Elijah's faith. God gave the command so that He could fulfill the promise. It is as if He said to His prophet, "I want you to go to the brook because My gifts are waiting for you there." In the same way, when God says, "Take, eat; . . . drink of it," He does not concern Himself with your eating and drinking so much as He concerns Himself with the promise He attached to your eating and drinking: "this is . . . for the forgiveness of sins." By way of another example, think about how a parent might say to his college-aged child,

"Meet me today at noon and we'll have lunch together." Certainly the child's act of meeting the parent is obedience in response to a command, but the promise attached to the command gives the command value: "we'll have lunch together." In the same way, God gives commands to His people, not merely to demand their obedient acts, but to lavish upon them the riches of His grace. Thus His command to "Take, eat; . . . drink of it," is much like the command He gave to Elijah, "Hide yourself by the brook Cherith." In each case, God attaches a promise and a miracle to the requirement.

What phrase does 1 Kings 17:5 use to describe Elijah's faith and trust in God? How does this compare to Acts 2:42?

"So he went and did according to the word of the LORD" (1 Kings 17:5). This is similar to how the early Christians behaved in the Book of Acts. They did not wonder why they should eat bread and wine; they did not question the value of Holy Communion or whether they should have it weekly or every other Sunday. They simply "devoted themselves to the apostles' teaching and fellowship, to the breaking of bread [a reference to Holy Communion] and the prayers" (Acts 2:42).

Does any other passage of the Old Testament come to mind when you think about the miraculous way God provided for Elijah in the wilderness? See Exodus 16:13–15. What similarities can you see in these two events? What comforts do these two miracles offer you?

Bread and meat came from heaven for Elijah in a way that is somewhat similar to the manna and quail that God provided to Israel in the wilderness. In each case, similarities include (1) the provision of bread where there is none, (2) extreme hunger, (3) birds, and (4) the ongoing nature of each miracle. Yet even greater than all of these, the two miracles are similar in that God keeps special watch and care for those whom He loves. The gracious and fatherly love God displays in these two miracles caused Mary later to sing, "He [God] has filled the hungry with good things, . . . He has helped His servant Israel" (Luke 1:53–54). Martin Luther commented on this portion of Mary's song by remembering the ravens at the Cherith brook:

> *"He has filled the hungry with good things." It is utterly impossible for God to let anyone who trusts in Him die of starvation; all angels would have to come and feed him. Elijah was fed by ravens and lived for many days on a handful of meal, he and the widow of Zarephath (1 Kings 17:6, 15). God cannot forsake those who trust in Him. Hence David says in Psalm 37:25: "I have been young, and now am old; yet I have not seen the righteous forsaken, or his children begging bread."* (AE *21:346–47)*

According to Luther, it goes against God's nature ever to let His children starve. However, it also goes against our fallen nature to believe it and trust in Him for our daily bread.

> *But our wretched unbelief always hinders God from working such works in us, and ourselves from experiencing and knowing them. We desire to be filled and have plenty of everything before hunger and want arrive. We lay up provision against future hunger and need, so that we no longer have need of God and His works. What sort of faith is that which trusts in God, when all the while you feel and know that you have goods laid up to help yourself? It is because of our unbelief that we see God's Word, the truth, and the right defeated and wrong triumph and yet remain silent, do not rebuke, speak out, or prevent it, but let things go as they will. Why? We are afraid that we, too, might be attacked and made poor and might then perish of hunger and be forever laid low. That is to esteem temporal goods more than God and to put them in God's place as an idol. If we do this, we do not deserve to hear or to understand this comfortable promise of God: that He exalts the lowly, puts down the mighty, fills the poor, and empties the rich.* (AE *21:347)*

Against such persistent temptations, God gives us the example of Israel in the wilderness and of Elijah at the brook Cherith, in order that we may know and never doubt that He truly regards and watches over each of His beloved children. As the Lord provided for each of these in the Old Testament, so shall He faithfully provide for the needs of His dear children today.

Miraculous Measure

What happened to Elijah in 1 Kings 17:7? Does this mean that God forgot about His servant, or that He was no longer caring for Elijah?

Because the drought became so severe, the brook Cherith dried up. Elijah's source of water was now gone. But God had not forgotten about His servant! He simply chose a different way of providing for Elijah's needs, just as He chose a new way of providing for Israel's needs after the people entered into the land of Canaan (see Joshua 5:12). The ravens and the brook were replaced by the widow of Zarephath, through whom God continued to care for Elijah.

This verse, which speaks about the drying of the brook, calls all Christians to greater faith and trust in the God who promises daily bread. Just as the Lord saw fit to dry up the brook, so also today He occasionally sees fit to take away the things He uses to care for His people. Examples might include the loss of a job, a debilitating injury, or the loss of a parent or spouse. Yet God faithfully provides His people with a replacement for that which He takes away. Just as the ravens and the brook were replaced by the widow of Zarephath, so the loss of a job might be replaced for a while by an unemployment check; an injury might be answered by a new job that does not require physical labor. A child's loss of a parent might be answered by a relative or friend who takes the child into his home and cares for him. The comfort that God speaks to His people during times of loss and misfortune is summarized by King David, who declared in the psalm, "Cast your burden on the LORD, and He will sustain you; He will never permit the righteous to be moved" (Psalm 55:22).

Discuss some of the things that Elijah might have been thinking as he watched his water supply dry up and disappear. He no longer had any food or water, but what did he still possess? In what way did God continue to provide for Elijah, according to 1 Kings 17:8–16?

There are many possible answers to what Elijah might have been thinking as he watched the flowing stream turn to a trickle of water, then to dry and bare rock. He may have thought, "I'll probably die!" and "What is God doing to me?" and "What have I done to deserve this?"

Still, even after the brook went dry, Elijah had God's promise that He would care for His servant: "Go to Zarephath, which belongs to Sidon, and dwell there. Behold, I have commanded a widow there to feed you" (1 Kings 17:9). At this Word from the Lord, a person of lesser faith would have been confronted by a whole new batch of tempting thoughts! Why would God send me to a Gentile territory, rather than keep me here in the land He gave to my people? Why would He choose a helpless widow to feed me—I am probably much more able-bodied and much more able to provide food than she is!

Yet Elijah took every thought captive (2 Corinthians 10:5), and he listened to the word and promise of God, as strange as that word and promise might have sounded to him.

What command does Elijah speak to the widow of Zarephath in 1 Kings 17:13–14? Is this command Elijah's own word, or does he speak on behalf of someone else? What promise is attached to this command?

Even though God had "commanded a widow there [in Zarephath]" (1 Kings 17:9) to feed Elijah, the widow did not seem to be aware of the command! Far from welcoming the traveling prophet with open arms, the widow was preparing herself and her son for death. They had only a small amount of oil and flour left, and they intended to "eat it and die" (1 Kings 17:12).

Even though the widow was not yet aware that God had chosen her to provide for Elijah, these verses bear witness to the power of God's preached Word. Elijah preached a sermon to the woman who believed herself about to die, and this preaching created faith and hope where there was once only despair and death:

Do not fear; go and do as you have said. But first make me a little cake of it and bring it to me, and afterward make something for yourself and your son. For thus says the LORD the God of Israel, "The jar of flour shall not be spent, and the jug of oil shall not be empty, until the day that the LORD sends rain upon the earth." (1 Kings 17:13–14)

How does the widow of Zarephath show that she has faith and trust in God?

It may not seem like that big of a deal for someone to mix flour and oil to make bread. But here is a great example of the sort of good works a Christian does! The widow's simple act of baking bread was carried out by faith. All she could see with her eyes was "only a handful of flour in a jar and a little oil in a jug." Yet the prophet's declaration of God's Word was attached to the flour and water: "For thus says the LORD the God of Israel, 'The jar of flour shall not be spent, and the jug of oil shall not be empty, until the day that the LORD sends rain upon the earth'" (1 Kings 17:14). Living by faith, the widow trusted more in what she heard with her ears than what she saw with her eyes. And God proved faithful: "The jar of flour was not spent, neither did the jug of oil become empty, according to the word of the LORD that He spoke by Elijah" (1 Kings 17:16).

Martin Luther used this woman's example as he preached about the great confidence and certainly Christians place in the promises of God:

Everything depends on our clinging to faith and prayer and on our taking comfort from the thought that God, who not only can increase a small supply through His blessing, as He marvelously and unexpectedly increased the flour and oil of the widow at Zarephath (1 Kings 17:16), but also can at will make everything out of nothing. (What Luther Says, *no. 1295)*

By way of a parallel, it would not be unfair to say that the bread and wine of Holy Communion have no special look about them. They are only bread and wine. Yet what miraculous thing happens to those who receive this small and simple meal?

Luther gives us a good answer in the Small Catechism: "These words, 'Given and shed for you for the forgiveness of sins,' show us that in the Sacrament forgiveness of sins, life, and salvation are given us through these words. For where there is forgiveness of sins, there is also life and salvation" (*SC*, pp. 29, 233).

Just as the widow's jar of flour and jug of oil miraculously provided life and salvation from the drought for her entire household, so also do the bread and wine of Holy Communion—a seemingly small and insignificant meal to the bare eye—provide life and salvation to all who believe in God's promise.

This miracle was not a single event, but essentially, God's act provided Elijah, the widow, and her son with a continual, unending meal. As often as they ate, they participated in God's ongoing act of salvation. In what way does this observation apply also to Holy Communion?

God's unwavering promise, attached to the widow's flour and oil, remained for the duration of the famine. Each and every time the widow went to the jug and jar for her family, she found sufficient provisions in keeping with God's promises. In the same way, God's unwavering promise is attached to the bread and wine of Holy Communion. Each and every time you approach the altar to receive this Sacrament, God unfailingly and miraculously provides for you the gifts that you need—forgiveness and life. Realizing this, perhaps it is not very helpful to ask, "How often should a Christian receive Holy Communion?" Perhaps the better question is, "How often are my pastor and congregation able to make God's great and precious meal of Holy Communion available to me?"

Conclusion

By returning again and again to the jar of flour and jug of oil (which reason and logic would never have believed still had flour and oil in them), Elijah, the widow, and her son were all proclaiming by their actions, "I believe that what God said is true. We need not worry! The oil and flour will not run out until this terrible famine ends!"

As 1 Corinthians 11:26 states, "For as often as you eat this bread and drink the cup, you proclaim the Lord's death until He comes." Rev. C. F. W. Walther, one of the founders of The Lutheran Church—Missouri Synod, once preached on this verse, calling Holy Communion "the pulpit of the laity." That is to say, your action of receiving Holy Communion is your opportunity to preach to the Church and the world the saving benefits of Christ's death and resurrection for your salvation. By attending Holy Communion, you proclaim these certainties (among other things):

*** Christ died for the sins of the whole world. Therefore, I know He died for my sins.**

*** The benefits of Christ's death and resurrection are served here in bread and wine.**

*** I am a sinner, needing the benefits of Christ's death and resurrection.**

*** I believe that here Christ is truly present in bread and wine, serving me forgiveness of sins, life, and salvation.**

Closing Prayer

Feed your children, God most holy,
Comfort sinners poor and lowly;
You our Bread of Life from heaven,
Bless the food You here have given!
As these gifts the body nourish,
May our souls with graces flourish
Till with saints in heav'nly splendor
At your feast our thanks we render.

Johann Heermann, 1585–1647; tr. *The Lutheran Hymnal,* 1941, alt. (*LW* 468)

My Cup Overflows

Elijah and the Widow

Bird Food

What sermon did Elijah preach to King Ahab in **1 Kings 17:1**?

According to **1 Kings 16:29–34**, what evil had Ahab done? Who else was included in the drought God visited on Ahab?

God then gave Elijah special instructions in **1 Kings 17:2–4**. What command does God speak? What promise did He attach to His command?

In what way might this "promise attached to a command" that God spoke to Elijah help us to understand Jesus' commands in **Matthew 26:26–28**?

What phrase does **1 Kings 17:5** use to describe Elijah's faith and trust in God? How does this compare to **Acts 2:42**?

Does any other passage of the Old Testament come to mind when you think about the miraculous way God provided for Elijah in the wilderness? See **Exodus 16:13–15**. What similarities can you see in these two events? What comforts do these two miracles offer you?

Miraculous Measure

What happened to Elijah in **1 Kings 17:7**? Does this mean that God forgot about His servant, or that He was no longer caring for Elijah?

Discuss some of the things that Elijah might have been thinking as he watched his water supply dry up and disappear. He no longer had any food or water, but what did he still possess? In what way did God continue to provide for Elijah, according to **1 Kings 17:8–16**?

What command does Elijah speak to the widow of Zarephath in **1 Kings 17:13–14**? Is this command Elijah's own word, or does he speak on behalf of someone else? What promise is attached to this command?

How does the widow of Zarephath show that she has faith and trust in God?

By way of a parallel, it would not be unfair to say that the bread and wine of Holy Communion have no special look about them. They are only bread and wine. Yet what miraculous thing happens to those who receive this small and simple meal?

This miracle was not a single event, but essentially, God's act provided Elijah, the widow, and her son with a continual, unending meal. As often as they ate, they participated in God's ongoing act of salvation. In what way does this observation apply also to Holy Communion?

5

Crumbs for the Children

Food in Matthew's Gospel

Lesson Focus

"Even the dogs eat the crumbs that fall from their masters' table" (Matthew 15:27). This lesson will focus on the prominence of food—bread, in particular—in Matthew's Gospel. The Sermon on the Mount sends the hearer in the right direction, emphasizing that bread in this Gospel means more than mere physical sustenance. The feeding miracles show how Christ miraculously provided for His hearer's hunger and thirst for righteousness. Between the feeding of the five thousand and the feeding of the four thousand, a Canaanite woman observes that even the tiniest morsel of the supernatural bread that Jesus gives is able to satisfy.

Note: The vast majority of the thoughts expressed in this lesson are drawn from a recent book written by seminary professor David Scaer. In his *Discourses in Matthew: Jesus Teaches the Church* (CPH, 2004), Dr. Scaer provides some delightful insights into the topic at hand. Many of these insights are documented here by quotations from his book. Many others have simply found their way into the questions and answers of this session. For this, I am indebted and grateful to my professor, who continues to open God's Word for me even years after my seminary graduation.

Introduction

Ask the students if any of them have ever watched or participated in an eating contest. How much food was consumed? Or, how many students have been so hungry at a meal that they went back for a second, third, or fourth portion of food?

One way the Bible describes our need for salvation is by the image of hunger, "Blessed are those who hunger and thirst for righteousness, for they shall be satisfied" (Matthew 5:6). The promise "they shall be satisfied" does not refer only to a great, future day in heaven, when all needs are completely fulfilled, but also to the gifts God gives to His people today. As Christians gather to eat and drink Holy Communion, the resurrected and ascended Lord, Jesus Christ, feeds them His body and blood, already beginning to satisfy their hunger and thirst for righteousness. They do not need to feast on huge amounts of bread and wine, for a small morsel and a tiny taste of the body and blood of the Lord are more than sufficient to fill the sinner's need. This is not merely an occasional meal! Just as the body needs a regular supply of food for its nourishment and health, so also Christians need God's regular and ongoing gift of Holy Communion for the nourishment that leads to eternal life.

Opening Prayer

May our dear Lord God help us to learn this lesson well, so that with our whole heart we firmly believe his Word and promises, and through Christ, with the Holy Spirit's help, are eternally saved. Amen. (Sermons of Martin Luther, *p. 328)*

Crowds

What sort of hunger does Jesus speak about in Matthew 5:6? In what way might this verse shape your understanding of Matthew 6:11? How about your understanding of any other references to food or to eating in this Gospel?

In Matthew 5:6, the fourth Beatitude, Jesus speaks about "those who hunger and thirst for righteousness. This refers not merely to physical hunger that is satisfied by filling the belly, but to spiritual hunger that can only be satisfied by God, who will satisfy the longing of saints for righteousness." Jesus' words seem to echo what David prayed in the psalms, when he wrote about being satisfied by seeing the likeness of God (Psalm 17:15) and when he anticipated how his "soul will be satisfied as with fat and rich food" (Psalm 63:5) by remembering the salvation that God has provided for him. "The hungering and thirsting suggest that a person's total existence is dependent for life upon something outside of him" (*The Sermon on the Mount,* p. 85).

This reference to spiritual fulfillment and satisfaction should alert us to the possibility that other references to food throughout Matthew's Gospel might involve something more than mere eating and drinking. Interestingly, the next reference to food after the fourth Beatitude is the Fourth Petition of the Lord's Prayer (Matthew 6:11). Those who have just heard assurances that God will satisfy their hunger and thirst for righteousness may confidently pray for their daily bread, knowing they shall be satisfied. Realizing that physical bread is not nearly as important as "every word that comes from the mouth of God" (Matthew 4:4), the request for daily bread in the Lord's Prayer likely looks beyond mere food that goes into the mouth. We might even say that the Fourth Petition is faith's response to the fourth Beatitude. Certainly included here is "everything that has to do with the support and needs of the body" (*SC,* pp. 18, 185). But also included are the needs of the spirit, "Ultimately, it has to do with a nourishment for a higher, more permanent life than what is experienced by everyone here on earth" (*Discourses in Matthew,* pp. 181–82).

Read about Jesus' well-known miracle of feeding the five thousand in Matthew 14:13–21. According to the verses just prior to this reading, what event did Jesus hear about that caused Him to withdraw into the wilderness? What significance might this setting add to Jesus' miracle?

Jesus withdrew into "a desolate place by Himself" (Matthew 14:13) after He heard about John the Baptizers' death at the hands of Herod Antipas (Matthew 14:8–12). There are probably several reasons for our Lord's self-isolation, not the least of which are (a) grief over the loss of a blood-relative (Luke 1:36); (b) Jesus' recognition that John was the last of the great Old Testament prophets (Matthew 11:7–11); and (c) Jesus' knowledge that John's death brought Him closer to His own suffering and death (Matthew 16:21). Jesus' withdrawal into a desolate place illustrates that when Christ became man, He truly took upon Himself every aspect of our human nature, including its frailties. "He was . . . a man of sorrows, and acquainted with grief" (Isaiah 53:3). Jesus did not use His divine nature to insulate Himself against heartbreak, anguish, or pain. Rather, He allowed Himself to suffer everything that we suffer—including the loss of loved ones and the fear of death—in order that He might defeat for us everything that makes us grieve or feel afraid.

Jesus' self-isolation also sets the stage for the miracle recorded in Matthew 14:13–21. Even when grieving, Jesus was not allowed the comforts of solitude because the crowds heard about His departure and "they followed Him on foot from the towns" (v. 13). Ever the faithful Shepherd, our Lord did not allow His own needs to stand in the way of caring for His neighbor's need: "When He went ashore He saw a great crowd, and He had compassion on them and healed their sick" (v. 14). Here in this "desolate place," with no food or water available, the stage is set for Jesus to miraculously feed "about five thousand men, besides women and children" (v. 21).

In what way might the following verses help lead those who hear Matthew's Gospel into a deeper understanding of this miraculous meal? Matthew 2:14–15; 4:1–4; 8:5–13

The feeding of the five thousand is one of the high points in Matthew's Gospel, especially when you are studying how Matthew includes the use of food in teaching about God's salvation through Christ Jesus. However, these other verses help to prepare Matthew's hearers for a deeper understanding of this important miracle.

In Matthew 2:14–15, Joseph took Jesus and His mother to Egypt. This journey to Egypt provided an escape from Herod the Great, who jealously killed the young boys of Bethlehem in his desire to destroy King Jesus. A second purpose for the trip to Egypt, however, "was to fulfill what the Lord had spoken by the prophet, 'Out of Egypt I called My son'" (Matthew 2:15). Citing Hosea 11:1, Matthew alerts his predominantly Jewish hearers to the Old Testament significance to Christ's life, death, and resurrection for our salvation.

> *Foundational in understanding this citation [Hosea 11:1] is Israel's liberation from Egypt, through which the children of Israel became God's people (son). Here is a word of grace. In view is the entire history of Israel from its entrance into Egypt to the people's reluctance to follow Moses back to Canaan. Within the Hosea citation, the message of the entire Torah (Pentateuch [that is, the first five books of the Old Testament]) is compressed. Part of this com-*

ing "out of Egypt" was the annual Passover celebration, which made the ancient event a present reality for the people. (Discourses in Matthew, *p.177)*

Matthew's reference to Egypt in 2:14–15 helps prepare the hearer for the feeding of the five thousand by lending significance to the "desolate place" (Matthew 14:13) where this miracle happened. This wilderness scene creates a memory of Israel's similar wilderness experience in the days of the exodus, during which the large group of people must look to God and to God alone for bread. Both in the exodus and in the feeding of the five thousand, God graciously provides.

In Matthew 4:1–4, the devil's temptation of Jesus leads the hearer to realize that Jesus is certainly more than able to create bread. At stake is not really the question of whether Jesus is able, but whether Jesus will act to meet His own personal needs. In answer to the devil's temptations, Jesus contents Himself to live on "every word that comes from the mouth of God" (Matthew 4:4). Yet the very same thing He refused to do for Himself in the wilderness (Matthew 4), Jesus willingly does for the crowds in the "desolate place" (Matthew 14)! In this way, Matthew depicts Jesus as the God who "came not to be served but to serve" (Matthew 20:28).

Matthew 8:5–13 tells about the centurion who asked Jesus to heal his ill servant. Jesus commended the centurion's willingness simply to hear the divine word, rather than have Jesus come to his house: "Truly, I tell you, with no one in Israel have I found such faith. I tell you, many will come from east and west and recline at table with Abraham, Isaac, and Jacob in the kingdom of heaven" (vv. 10–11). This centurion indicates that Gentiles will be included in the divine meal that satisfies "those who hunger and thirst for righteousness" (Matthew 5:6).

In the Sermon on the Mount, Matthew taught his catechumens to dismiss their concerns about ordinary food; now he focuses on a meal that transcends time and space, a meal that even crosses Israel's borders. "The meal in which the Gentiles will participate lies in the future. In the accounts of the feeding of the four and five thousand, this banqueting begins to occur" (*Discourses in Matthew*, p. 184).

So Jesus prophesies that the Gentiles will participate in the great, messianic feast of salvation that God prepares for His people (Matthew 8:11). Then, in the feeding of the five thousand (Matthew 14:13–21) and four thousand (Matthew 15:32–39), He anticipates this feast by miraculously providing food for those whose hunger and thirst have driven them to Him.

What comes to mind when you read the verbs that describe Jesus' actions in Matthew 14:19? Compare them to the same verbs in Matthew 26:26.

For those who are familiar with the words of institution for Holy Communion, Jesus' actions in Matthew 14:19–20 bring the sacrament to mind. "Taking the five loaves and the two fish, He looked up to heaven and said a blessing. Then He broke the loaves and gave them to the disciples, and the disciples gave them to the crowds." The same verbs are used when Jesus gave His disciples Holy Communion: "Jesus took bread, and after blessing it broke it and gave it to the disciples" (Matthew 26:26). This similarity in word usage deliberately draws a connection between the feeding of the five thousand and the institution of Holy Communion. While we would not necessarily say that Jesus gave the five thousand Holy Communion, we certainly could conclude that Holy Communion is as miraculous a meal for us as the feeding of the five thousand was for those who were present. In each case, the God-Man Jesus provides nourishment for body and soul.

In what way does Matthew 14:16 get fulfilled by verses 19–20? Is there any application that can be made to the Church's celebration of Holy Communion today?

In Matthew 14:16, Jesus commanded His disciples, "You give them something to eat." Over their protests that they have only five loaves and two fish to give, Jesus miraculously provides them with food to serve to His people. "Then He broke the loaves and gave them to the disciples, and the disciples gave them to the crowds."

In the same way, Holy Communion is not something that the pastor provides for the people of God, but it is a miraculous meal that Christ provides. The Lutheran Church's earliest confessional document taught—and we still believe today—that "no one should publicly teach in the Church, or administer the Sacraments, without a rightly ordained call" (*Concordia,* AC, XIV). The feeding of the five thousand shows that Holy Communion is not the pastor's personal possession to do with as he pleases, but that he is called to administer the Sacraments that belong to Jesus and are given to the Church. To "administer the Sacraments" is not to own them, but to manage, to oversee, and to act in place of the giver of this meal. Just as Jesus gave the miraculous fish and bread to the people through the distribution worked by the disciples, so also does Jesus give the Sacrament of Holy Communion to the Church through the Office of the Ministry.

Psalm 23 has always been a popular psalm for God's people, even in Jesus' day. What small detail does the evangelist Mark add to his version of the feeding of the five thousand, which brings this important psalm to mind? See Mark 6:39.

Where Matthew wrote that Jesus instructed the people to "sit down on the grass" (14:19), Mark adds the seemingly minor detail, "then He [Jesus] commanded them all to sit down in groups on the green grass" (6:39). The addition of the word *green* evokes the memory of Psalm 23, which was a dearly loved psalm even two thousand years ago. By adding this word, Mark opens the door to realizing that this miraculous meal was God's act of protecting the crowds who were "like sheep without a shepherd" (Mark 6:34). But here in the feeding of the five thousand—which is echoed in Holy Communion—God "makes [His people] lie down in green pastures" (Psalm 23:2), safe and secure from the enemies all around.

What particular aspects of Psalm 23 provide helpful details to (a) the feeding of the five thousand and (b) the Lord's Supper?

By bringing to mind Psalm 23 in his report of the feeding the five thousand, Mark allows the hearer to realize that this miracle took place "in the presence of my enemies" (Psalm 23:5). This is true because the feeding of the five thousand took place immediately after King Herod's execution of John the Baptizer, the faithful preacher of God's Word. King Herod shows himself to be an enemy of God's people, for he hates the divine Word that God speaks. Yet in the feeding of the five thousand, Jesus offers rest and protection from all enemies—King Herod included.

In a similar way, Holy Communion is rightly understood as "a table before me in the presence of my enemies" (Psalm 23:5). What enemies can oppose and overcome you here? Sin is forgiven in the blood of Christ, "poured out for many" (Matthew 26:28); death is destroyed where sin is forgiven; where sins are forgiven, "the accuser" (Revelation 12:10) is thrown down—he has nothing left to accuse! "They have conquered him by the blood of the Lamb" (Revelation 12:11).

After the feeding of the five thousand, Matthew tells about another, similar miracle in which four thousand were fed. See Matthew 15:29–39. Why might Matthew have included reports on both miracles, rather than only one? Compare Exodus 16:35.

In Exodus 16:35, Moses reports that the people of "Israel ate the manna forty years, till they came to a habitable land." That is to say, God miraculously provided for His people in a continual way, not just on one occasion. Similarly, the feeding of the four thousand indicates that Jesus continually cares for the needs of His people, whom He loves. Notice that the variation in details is only minor: there are four thousand in the second miracle, rather than five; there are "seven loaves and a few small fish" (Matthew 15:34) instead of "five loaves and two fish" (Matthew 14:17); seven baskets of leftovers were gathered instead of twelve. These differences are important, because they indicate two separate miracles, rather than a repeated telling of the same miracle.

The similarities between these two miracles are equally important. These include the great need of the people; Jesus' compassion (Matthew 14:14; 15:32); seating the crowd on the ground; the communion-like actions of taking, giving thanks, breaking, and giving; the apostolic distribution to the people; "and they all ate and were satisfied" (Matthew 14:20; 15:37).

Clearly, Matthew regards Jesus' miraculous treatment of bread to be important enough to mention it twice.

> *If the second feeding were eliminated, the crescendo or momentum created by the evangelist for his hearers would be lost. Upon hearing the feeding of the five thousand, catechumens may have been tempted to consider the account to be simply another discourse on divine providence . . . that is, God simply takes care of us. The temptation to trivialize the miracle is overcome by placing a second feeding almost immediately after the first.* (Discourses in Matthew, *p. 187)*

The connection between these miracles and the miraculous meal of Holy Communion must not be missed! Matthew emphasizes this important connection by reporting two miraculous feedings, rather than only one. Mark (6:30–44; 8:1–10) does likewise.

Crumbs

Between the feeding of the five thousand and the feeding of the four thousand, there is the story of the Canaanite woman who came to Jesus. See Matthew 15:21–28. What is this woman's opinion of Jesus, expressed in verse 22?

This woman recognizes that Jesus is the Messiah sent from God, the Promised One about whom the Old Testament prophets spoke. By calling Him "Lord, Son of David" (Matthew 15:22), this woman indicates that she is a pious believer, even though she is a Gentile.

Who are the children in verse 26? Who are the dogs? Do Jesus' words in this passage seem loving and compassionate?

When Jesus says, "It is not right to take the children's bread" (Matthew 15:26), He is referring to the Jews, whom He also calls "the lost sheep of the house of Israel" (v. 24). The "dogs" are the Gentiles, that is, everyone who is not Jewish. This woman is an "outsider," and one who lives in the presence of demons, at that! Yet this woman also provides us with great comfort, because she feels willing to approach Jesus, the Son of God, and make her requests known to Him. She reveals that no one needs first to "clean up their act" or "get right with God" before they can approach Jesus. She simply comes to Him with all her struggles and difficulties, and lays them at Jesus' feet.

Jesus' words, "It is not right to take the children's bread and throw it to the dogs" (Matthew 15:26) sound harsh and condemning, but it must be remembered that this is God's merciful and loving Son speaking! Jesus does not say these words in order to drive this woman away, but to sharpen her faith. As Martin Luther explains, Jesus' harsh words give the woman opportunity not to run away from Him but to cling all the more to His grace and mercy:

> *Faith takes Christ captive in His word . . . Thus she [the Canaanite woman] catches Christ with His own words, and He is happy to be caught. "Very well," she says, "if I am a dog, I ask no more than a dog's rights. I am not a child nor am I of Abraham's seed, but You are a rich Lord and set a lavish table. Give Your children the bread and a place at the table; I do not wish that. Let me, merely a dog, pick up the crumbs under the table, allowing me that which the children don't need or even miss, the crumbs, and I will be content therewith." So she catches Christ, the Lord, in His own words and with that wins not only the right of a dog, but also that of the children. Now then where will He go, our dear Jesus? He let Himself be made a captive, and must comply. Be sure of this: that's what He most deeply desires.* (Sermons of Martin Luther, *p. 325)*

Take a closer look at the details in the story of the Canaanite woman. See if there might be a hint or two in theses passages that brings Holy Communion to mind:

a. What verb does Jesus use in verse 26, when He speaks about bread? How does this compare with Matthew 14:19; 15:36; and 26:26?

Jesus says, "It is not right to take the children's bread and throw it to the dogs" (Matthew 15:26). He could have said, in a more simple way, "It is not right to throw the children's bread to the dogs." He also could have used a different word, such as "It is not right to grab the children's bread . . ." or "it is not right pick up the children's bread."

However, Jesus deliberately used the word *take,* a word that helped make the feeding of the five thousand (Matthew 14:19) and of the four thousand (Matthew 15:36) sound similar to the celebration of Holy Communion. In each case, and also at the Last Supper (Matthew 26:26), Jesus *takes* bread. When Jesus says to the woman, "It is not right to *take* the . . . bread" (Matthew 15:26), the word *take* "initiates an awareness of both the miraculous feedings and the Eucharist [Holy Communion]" (*Discourses in Matthew*, p, 191).

b. What comparison can you draw between verse 27 and 1 Corinthians 10:21?

In 1 Corinthians 10:21, the apostle Paul writes, "You cannot partake of the table of the Lord and the table of demons." Here, the "table of the Lord" refers to Holy Communion. This bears at least a similarity to the woman's words to Jesus, speaking about "their masters' table" (Matthew 15:27). The Greek word for "master" is *kurios,* the same word used for "Lord" in 1 Corinthians 10:21!

c. Where have you recently heard a similar reference to the leftover pieces of bread that are mentioned in verse 27? (Compare Matthew 14:20 and 15:37.)

Both of the feeding miracles that bracket this story of the Canaanite woman speak about the disciples gathering up "the broken pieces left over" (Matthew 14:20; 15:37). In other words, the disciples were gathering up crumbs. The woman recognizes that these crumbs are of great value, even though they are fragmented and small. This suggests that she understood that Jesus was not speaking about physical bread when He mentioned "the children's bread" (Matthew 15:26). Rather, He was speaking about the spiritual bread He provides for the nourishment of faith.

> *Her desire only for crumbs (15:27), not for a loaf, points to the woman's knowledge that the bread of which Jesus is speaking is supernatural. Leftover crumbs that no one cares about are as valuable as the bread itself; a crumb is as good as a loaf. Here the eucharistic parallel is amazing.* (Discourses in Matthew, *p. 192)*

Just as a mere "crumb" of Jesus' grace and mercy would satisfy the woman's need, so also do the small bits of bread and little sips of wine received in Communion fully provide each communicant with the full riches of forgiveness, life, and salvation. It matters not how much of the bread and wine you receive, but that you receive it in faith, as the Canaanite woman received Christ's mercy in faith. "Without anticipating, knowing about, or receiving the Eucharist, she has the faith required of catechumens for the reception of the Eucharist" (*Discourses in Matthew*, p. 192).

When Jesus gave Holy Communion to His disciples in Matthew 26:26–29, what small but important word did He use to describe the relationship between bread and His body, wine and His blood? Why is this word so important?

When Jesus said, "This is My body . . . this is My blood" (Matthew 26:26, 28), He used the Greek word that translates into the English *is.* This might not seem like a big deal at first, but the importance of this little word can hardly be overestimated. Many Christians today do not believe that Jesus meant *is* when He said "This is My body . . . this is My blood," but that He meant *symbolizes* or *represents.* The people who make these claims cannot accept that Jesus could possibly join His true body and blood—the same body and blood that were sacrificed on the cross, but now in a resurrected, glorified form—to something as plain, ordinary, and small as bread and wine.

The problem with such thinking is that it throws away the clear words of the Bible. If Jesus meant to say *symbolizes* or *represents,* there are specific Greek words that He could have used. (For example, Peter does this in 1 Peter 3:21.)

However, Jesus did not say "this symbolizes My body" or "this represents My blood." He emphatically said, "This *is* My body . . . this *is* My blood." Often, the verb *is* does not even appear in the Greek, but it is implied when two nouns are close together. For example, a Greek could simply write, "Jesus Lord" without writing the verb *is.* The verb is implied. Thus the phrase "Jesus Lord" in Greek would be translated into English as "Jesus is Lord" (1 Corinthians 12:3).

Because the verb *is* can be implied in Greek, its occurrence is pretty important. Jesus used the word *is* when He wanted to emphasize His point. For example, when He said, "I am the door" (John 10:9), He did not say, "I door," in usual Greek fashion. He used the verb *is,* in order to emphasize, "I *am* the door." In the same way, when Jesus says, "This *is* My body . . . this *is* My blood," He used the actual word *is,* emphasizing for us that the bread and wine of Holy Communion truly are His actual body and blood, joined to bread and wine in a miraculous and inexplicable way.

Some people wrongly assume that, because Jesus used the words "fruit of the vine" in Matthew 26:29, grape juice must be used for Holy Communion. But might there be a scriptural reason for Jesus' use of this phrase? Take a look at John 15:1–5. According to that passage, what/who is the vine? What, then, is meant by "fruit of the vine"?

Jesus says in Matthew 26:29, "I tell you I will not drink again of this fruit of the vine until that day when I drink it new with you in My Father's kingdom." Before we go running off to conclude that "fruit of the vine" must speak about grape juice rather than wine, we ought to consider the other Bible passages that speak in this manner. Specifically, Jesus says in John 15:1–5,

> *I am the true vine, and My Father is the vinedresser. Every branch of Mine that does not bear fruit He takes away, and every branch that does bear fruit He prunes, that it may bear more fruit. Already you are clean because of the word that I have spoken to you. Abide in Me, and I in you. As a branch cannot bear fruit by itself, unless it abides in the vine, neither can you, unless you abide in Me. I am the vine, you are the branches. Whoever abides in Me and I in him, he it is that bears much fruit, for apart from Me you can do nothing.*

So Jesus says, "I am the vine"—and He includes the Greek word for *is* to emphasize that He *is* the vine! Realizing this, we ought to understand His words in Matthew 26:29, "the fruit of the vine," to refer to His miraculous presence in Holy Communion rather than grape juice.

Speaking about Holy Communion, Jesus promises in Matthew 26:29 that He will "drink it new with you in My Father's kingdom." What help does Matthew 16:28 give you in understanding these words? According to Matthew 3:2 and 12:28, where is God's kingdom?

In Matthew 16:28, Jesus says, "Truly, I say to you, there are some standing here who will not taste death until they see the Son of Man coming in His kingdom." This, of course, does not speak about Christ's return on the Last Day. If that were the case, then either (1) Christ was mistaken, or (2) there are some apostles still alive somewhere in the world, even after two thousand years. But the kingdom that Christ is speaking about in this verse is the one that He established for us in His crucifixion, resurrection, and ascension. Therefore, when Christ says in Matthew 26:29 that He will drink "with you in My Father's kingdom," we need not think that He is talking about the Last Day. Rather, He is speaking about how He communes and fellowships with us at every celebration of Holy Communion.

> *On the cross the old era passes away and a new one is inaugurated that will change the character in which the Eucharist is celebrated. Anticipated sorrows of the cross are replaced with the continuous joys of resurrection. Jesus' next participation in the Eucharist will recall the cross, not anticipate it, as did the first."* (Discourses in Matthew, *pp, 194–95)*

God's kingdom need not be thought of as something far away and distant from us. Both John the Baptizer and Jesus speak about the Kingdom as being very close. As John prepared the way for Jesus' Baptism, he declared, "The kingdom of heaven is at hand" (Matthew 3:2). Jesus spoke about the kingdom of heaven as being "upon" those among whom the Holy Spirit does His work (Matthew 12:28). Martin Luther realized that God's kingdom was not a distant place, but it is found where God's Word is preached, believed, and taken to heart: "God's kingdom comes when our heavenly Father gives us His Holy Spirit, so that by His grace we believe His holy Word and lead godly lives here in time and there in eternity" (*SC,* pp. 18, 179).

Conclusion

By coming to us in Holy Communion, Jesus partially fulfills His departing promise to His disciples, "I am with you always" (Matthew 28:20). This is not merely a symbolic reminder of what Jesus did for us, but an actual participation in the crucifixion for our salvation! Here we receive the benefits of Christ's death, along with the promise of Christ's resurrection. In these little "crumbs" (Matthew 15:27), we receive the full benefit and blessing of God's grace, joined to bread and wine.

Closing Prayer

O Lord, we praise You, bless You and adore You,
In thanksgiving bow before You.
Here with Your body and Your blood You nourish
Our weak souls that they may flourish.
O Lord, have mercy!
May Your body, Lord, born of Mary,
That our sins and sorrows did carry,
And Your blood for us plead
In all trial, fear, and need:
O Lord, have mercy!

German folk hymn, 15th cent.; tr. *The Lutheran Hymnal,* 1941, alt. (*LW* 238:1)

CRUMBS FOR THE CHILDREN

FOOD IN MATTHEW'S GOSPEL

Crowds

What sort of hunger does Jesus speak about in **Matthew 5:6**? In what way might this verse shape your understanding of **Matthew 6:11**? How about your understanding of any other references to food or to eating in this Gospel?

Read about Jesus' well-known miracle of feeding the five thousand in **Matthew 14:13–21**. According to the verses just prior to this reading, what event did Jesus hear about that caused Him to withdraw into the wilderness? What significance might this setting add to Jesus' miracle?

In what way might the following verses help lead those who hear Matthew's Gospel into a deeper understanding of this miraculous meal? **Matthew 2:14–15; 4:1–4; 8:5–13**

What comes to mind when you read the verbs that describe Jesus' actions in **Matthew 14:19**? Compare them to the same verbs in **Matthew 26:26**.

In what way does **Matthew 14:16** get fulfilled by **verses 19–20**? Is there any application that can be made to the Church's celebration of Holy Communion today?

Psalm 23 has always been a popular psalm for God's people, even in Jesus' day. What small detail does the evangelist Mark add to his version of the feeding of the five thousand, which brings this important psalm to mind? See **Mark 6:39**.

What particular aspects of **Psalm 23** provide helpful details to (a) the feeding of the five thousand and (b) the Lord's Supper?

After the feeding of the five thousand, Matthew tells about another, similar miracle in which four thousand were fed. See **Matthew 15:29–39**. Why might Matthew have included reports on both miracles, rather than only one? Compare **Exodus 16:35**.

Crumbs

Between the feeding of the five thousand and the feeding of the four thousand, there is the story of the Canaanite woman who came to Jesus. See **Matthew 15:21–28.** What is this woman's opinion of Jesus, expressed in **verse 22**?

Who are the children in **verse 26**? Who are the dogs? Do Jesus' words in this passage seem loving and compassionate?

Take a closer look at the details in the story of the Canaanite woman. See if there might be a hint or two in theses passages that brings Holy Communion to mind:

a. What verb does Jesus use in **verse 26**, when He speaks about bread? How does this compare with **Matthew 14:19; 15:36;** and **26:26**?

b. What comparison can you draw between **verse 27** and **1 Corinthians 10:21**?

c. Where have you recently heard a similar reference to the leftover pieces of bread that are mentioned in **verse 27**? (Compare **Matthew 14:20** and **15:37**)

When Jesus gave Holy Communion to His disciples in **Matthew 26:26–29,** what small but important word did He use to describe the relationship between bread and His body, wine and His blood? Why is this word so important?

Some people wrongly assume that, because Jesus used the words "fruit of the vine" in **Matthew 26:29,** grape juice must be used for Holy Communion. But might there be a scriptural reason for Jesus' use of this phrase? Take a look at **John 15:1–5.** According to that passage, what/who is the vine? What, then, is meant by "fruit of the vine"?

Speaking about Holy Communion, Jesus promises in **Matthew 26:29** that He will "drink it new with you in My Father's kingdom." What help does **Matthew 16:28** give you in understanding these words? According to **Matthew 3:2** and **12:28,** where is God's kingdom?

6

THE ETERNAL FEAST

FOOD IN REVELATION

Lesson Focus

This lesson will look at some of the food references in the Book of Revelation, also taking into consideration how the imagery of Revelation finds its way into our hymnody for Holy Communion. While many people think of Revelation as speaking about future things, it also includes references to our current life in the Church. While this life may be unseen to the naked eye, as we gather to eat what appears to be only bread and wine, there is a great, unseen dimension to our participation in Holy Communion. There we gather before the throne of the Lamb "with angels and archangels and with all the company of heaven" (*LW,* p. 146). There, too, we receive a small foretaste of the great eternal feast of heaven, at which we shall be eternally nourished by the gracious Lamb of God, our Lord Jesus Christ.

Introduction

Ask the students what goes through their minds during worship when the congregation sings hymns. Do they participate in the singing? Do they sing the words without contemplating their meanings? Discuss different ways the hymns of the Church might be used apart from public worship during the week.

The hymnals of the Lutheran Church—Missouri Synod (*Lutheran Service Book, Lutheran Worship,* and *The Lutheran Hymnal*) also make great devotional tools. They call upon the rich imagery of the Scriptures—and in so doing, they teach the Scriptures to us. This session makes use of several hymns from *Lutheran Worship* that include references to the Book of Revelation.

Opening Prayer

Let this food your faith so nourish
That by love its fruit may flourish
And your neighbor learn from you
How much God's wondrous love can do. Amen.

John Hus, c. 1369–1415; tr. F. Samuel Janzow, b. 1913; (*LW* 236:9)

Breaking Bread

In Revelation 2:14, Jesus rebuked the Christians in the church of Pergamum for tolerating false teachers in their midst. Specifically, what error had become popular in this church? What major sins were associated with this error?

Jesus rebuked the Christians of Pergamum for tolerating those "who hold the teaching of Balaam" (Revelation 2:14), a false prophet in the Old Testament (see Numbers 22–24). The major sins associated with Balaam's error are eating food sacrificed to idols (i.e., participating in idol worship) and sexual immorality.

According to Numbers 25:1–2 and 31:16, what happened to those who originally tolerated this particular false teacher? What similar threat is made against the Christians of Pergamum in Revelation 2:16?

The Christians of Pergamum would do well to listen to the Scriptures, so that they may avoid the fate of the people of Israel, who committed adulterous acts with the daughters of Moab and "bowed down to their [Moabite] gods" (Numbers 25:2). As a result of their unbelieving acts, "the plague came among the congregation of the Lord" (Numbers 31:16). A similar threat was made against Pergamum: "Therefore repent. If not, I will come to you soon and war against them [the false teachers and those who tolerate them] with the sword of My mouth" (Revelation 2:16).

Long before John wrote Revelation, Paul wrote a letter to the Corinthians in which he also discussed food sacrificed to idols. John very well could have had Paul's letter in mind when he was writing Revelation 2:12–17. Compare 1 Corinthians 10:14–22. What gift from God does Paul simultaneously discuss when he addresses the topic of food sacrificed to idols?

When Paul calls upon the Corinthians to "flee from idolatry" and not to "drink the cup of the Lord and the cup of demons" (1 Corinthians 10:14, 21), he simultaneously discusses the miraculous meal of Holy Communion. The "cup of blessing that we bless" refers to the Communion cup, in which we have "a participation in the blood of Christ." Likewise, "the bread that we break" refers to the Communion bread, which is our "participation in the body of Christ" (1 Corinthians 10:16).

When Paul says "participation," the Greek word is *koinonia*, which is sometimes also translated into English as "fellowship." *Koinonia* refers to a very intimate connection between two things. For example, the Greeks sometimes used the word to describe the connection between a husband and wife, which the Bible also describes as "one flesh" (Genesis 2:24; Matthew 19:5–6; Ephesians 5:29–31) and one body (Ephesians 5:28). Therefore, when Paul says that Holy Communion gives us a "participation in the blood of Christ . . . in the body of Christ" (1 Corinthians 10:16), he describes an intimate, almost inexplicable connection between us and our Lord Jesus. For the Corinthians and the church at Pergamum to "participate" also in the feasts that celebrated idol sacrifices was for them to commit an act of spiritual adultery, unfaithfulness to Jesus, the true husband of the Church (Ephesians 5:25–32).

The early Lutherans realized that this word, *participation,* provides a powerful argument for our belief that Christ is not merely symbolized or represented in Holy Communion, but that He is truly present in the elements of bread and wine. In the Formula of Concord, these Lutherans confessed,

> *This is what is taught in the Augsburg Confession from God's Word about the Lord's Supper: "That the body and blood of Christ are truly present and distributed to those who eat the Lord's Supper" (AC X 1). The contrary doctrine is rejected. . . . This opinion is clear expressed in Luther's Small Catechism in the following words: What is the Sacrament of the Altar? Answer: It is the true body and blood of our Lord Jesus Christ, under the bread and wine, for us Christians to eat and to drink, instituted by Christ Himself (SC VI 1–2). In the Apology this is not only explained still more clearly, but is also established by the passage from Paul (1 Corinthians 10:16).* (Concordia *FC SD VII 9–10)*

Now return to Revelation 2:12–17. To those in the church of Pergamum who conquer (i.e., who remain faithful to the Word of God), what promise is spoken to them in Revelation 2:17? Is this promise spoken only to them? What Old Testament event does this promise call to mind?

Jesus promises, "To the one who conquers I will give some of the hidden manna, and I will give him a white stone, with a new name written on the stone that no one knows except the one who receives it" (Revelation 2:17). Of course, the reference to manna recalls Israel's wilderness journey, during which God miraculously provided them with manna from heaven. This promise applies to all believers.

What is meant by the word "hidden" in Revelation 2:17? To what might the phrase "hidden manna" possibly refer?

For something to be "hidden" means that it is present, but unseen. For example, if I am searching for my shoes, they might be present in the closet under a pile of other shoes. It's not that they are missing from the closet; it is simply that I cannot see them with my eyes.

When Jesus is talking about "hidden manna," He is speaking about miraculous food that cannot be discerned with the bare eye. While Bible scholars debate whether John is truly speaking about Holy Communion, these words at least bring the Sacrament to mind. In Communion, all we see with our eyes is bread and wine. Yet "hidden" in the bread and wine is the body and blood of Jesus, the "bread of life" (John 6:35) and the "true bread out of heaven" (John 6:32).

> *To him that conquers and overcomes all the tribulations and perils that best his path the Lord will give heavenly food, hidden manna, John 6:31–35, Christ Himself being that true spiritual food which meets every need of the soul. As we truly receive Christ and all His blessings through the means of grace here in time, so we shall afterward, in heaven, on the eternal Sabbath, enjoy His glory in its very fullness.* (Popular Commentary, *p. 598)*

Some scholars say that Revelation 2:17 gives no clear indication that "hidden manna" refers to Holy Communion. Many people say the same thing about John 6:22–59. Read through that passage, focusing especially on verses 35, 48–51, and 53–58. Without deciding definitively whether or not this passage is about Holy Communion, is it possible at least to say that Jesus' words here sound similar to those used in Holy Communion, or remind us of Holy Communion?

At the very least, John 6 brings Holy Communion to mind, especially when Jesus says such things as these: "I am the bread of life; whoever comes to me shall not hunger, and whoever believes in me shall never thirst" (v. 35). "Your fathers ate the manna in the wilderness, and they died" (v. 49). "I am the living bread that came down from heaven. If anyone eats of this bread, he will live forever. And the bread that I will give for the life of the world is my flesh" (v. 51). "Whoever feeds on My flesh and drinks My blood has eternal life, and I will raise him up on the last day. For My flesh is true food, and My blood is true drink. Whoever feeds on My flesh and drinks My blood abides in Me, and I in him" (vv. 54–56).

What do the following two hymn stanzas have to say about John 6:22–59?

Now in faith I humbly ponder
Over this surpassing wonder
That the bread of life is boundless
Though the souls it feeds are countless:
With the choicest wine of heaven
Christ's own blood to us is given.
Oh, most glorious consolation,
Pledge and seal of my salvation.

Johann Franck, 1618–77; tr. *Lutheran Book of Worship*, 1978. (*LW* 239:3)

Lutheran Worship and *The Lutheran Hymnal*, two of the officially recognized hymnals for The Lutheran Church—Missouri Synod, each contain this hymn in the section on the Lord's Supper (239 and 305, respectively). Using the imagery of John 6, this hymn brings Holy Communion to mind by speaking about "the bread of life" (compare John 6:35, 48), which is given with "Christ's own blood." *The Handbook for the Lutheran Hymnal* states,

> *This hymn is perhaps the finest of all German hymns for the Holy Communion. It is an exhortation to the soul to arise and draw near to partake of the Heavenly Food and to meditate on the wonders of the Heavenly Love, ending with a prayer for final reception at the Eternal Feast. It soon attained, and still retains, popularity in Germany (in many German churches it is still the unvarying hymn at the celebrations). (P. 219)*

O living Bread from heaven,
How well You feed Your guest!
The gifts that You have given
Have filled my heart with rest.
Oh, wondrous food of blessing,
Oh, cup that heals our woes!
My heart, this gift possessing,
With praises overflows.

Johann Rist, 1606–67; tr. Catherine Winkworth, 1829–78, alt. (*LW* 244:1)

Again, the imagery from John 6 is evident in this hymn that speaks about "living bread that came down from heaven" (John 6:51). This hymn also appears in both *Lutheran Worship* (244) and *The Lutheran Hymnal* (316). It describes how the bread from heaven feeds the "guest" at Holy Communion, that is, the communicant.

The Great Feast

Take a look at Revelation 3:20. Some Christians misuse this verse by claiming that, before we can be saved, we must first open up our heart and ask Jesus to come in. What clues can you spot in Revelation 3:14–21 that suggest that this passage is *not* speaking about God's gift of conversion?

Many false teachers use this verse in their preaching to insist that, before you can be saved, you must open the door of your heart and let Jesus in. After all, Christ Himself says in Revelation 3:20, "Behold, I stand at the door and knock. If anyone hears My voice and opens the door, I will come in to him and eat with him, and he with Me." However, such an approach to this passage, and directed toward the unsaved, both ignores other Scripture passages and neglects the context of Jesus' words in Revelation 2.

Other Scripture passages make it clear that, because people are dead in trespasses and sins (Ephesians 2:1) and hostile toward God (Romans 8:7), it is impossible for anyone to "choose" to "open the door of their heart." People become Christian in a way very similar to how Lazarus became alive again (John 11:38–44). Just as the powerful, life-giving Word of Jesus raised Lazarus up from the dead before Lazarus could respond and come out, so also God's powerful Word raises people up from their sins before they can "open" any doors to their hearts! Revelation 3:20 ought not be used as a way of exhorting people to "ask Jesus into their hearts"!

Plus, there is an important clue in Revelation 3:14–21 that helps us to realize that Jesus is not speaking about conversion when He says, "I stand . . . knock . . . opens the door." These words were written "to the angel of the church in Laodicea" (Revelation 3:14). That is to say, this letter about Jesus knocking on the door is written to Christians, to those into whom Christ already had come! These Christians had become enticed by the affairs of life. Their faith had become "lukewarm" and they had begun to push Jesus away, saying, "I am rich, I have prospered, and I need nothing" (Revelation 3:17). By ignoring Jesus and His Word, they did not even realize that they were "wretched, pitiable, poor, blind, and naked" (Revelation 3:17).

So Jesus calls these Christians to repentance again: "Behold, I stand at the door and knock. If anyone hears My voice and opens the door, I will come in to him and eat with him, and he with Me" (Revelation 3:20).

What surprising application of Revelation 3:20 is made in the following stanza of "Soul Adorn Yourself with Gladness," drawn from the section on the Lord's Supper in *Lutheran Worship*?

Hasten as a bride to meet Him,
Eagerly and gladly greet Him.
There he stands already knocking;
Quickly, now, your gate unlocking,
Open wide the fast-closed portal,
Saying to the Lord immortal:
"Come, and leave your loved one never;
Dwell within My heart forever."

Johann Franck, 1618–77; tr. *Lutheran Book of Worship,* 1978. (*LW* 239:2)

Drawing on the imagery of Christ coming in and eating with the Christian, this hymn applies Revelation 3:20 to Holy Communion! As Christians approach the body and blood of the Lord in Holy Communion, Jesus stands there "knocking," ready to enter into them through bread and wine, dwelling in their hearts forever. Those who believe in these words, "Given and shed for you for the forgiveness of sins," have their heart's door opened already. However, if you doubt these words or disbelieve them, your heart's door is barred and locked against Jesus when you come to Holy Communion. Repentance involves listening to the words of Jesus and believing them. In this way, you respond to His knocking, "quickly, now, your gate unlocking."

Read Revelation 19:6–9. What great event is described here? Who is included in this event?

In Revelation 19:6–9, John describes "the marriage supper of the Lamb" (Revelation 19:9). Those who take part in this event include "a great multitude" of saints (v. 6). Compare this statement with the words from the Preface to Holy Communion: "therefore with angels and archangels and with all the company of heaven" (*LW,* p. 146).

Bible scholars have noted that Matthew's Gospel was the most popular and widely used Gospel in the Early Church. It is likely to assume that John was familiar with Matthew's Gospel before he wrote Revelation. John may even have had Matthew's Gospel in mind when he wrote Revelation 19:6–9 in particular. Compare verse 9 to Matthew 22:1–14. According to verses 9–10 of the Matthew passage, who is invited to the Bridegroom's feast? Comparing Revelation

19:6, how many are included in this great invitation?

In Matthew 22, all people are invited to the wedding feast for the king's son. The invitation was first sent to the specially invited guests, none of whom wanted to attend the wedding. So then the king instructed his servants to include "as many as you can find" (v. 9). The servants went out and invited "all whom they found, both bad and good. So the wedding hall was filled with guests" (v. 10).

John, perhaps thinking about this passage from Matthew's Gospel, cannot even place a number on those "good and bad" (Matthew 22:10) who are numbered in the feast. He can only marvel that it was "a great multitude," so large that its voice of praise and thanksgiving before God sounded "like the roar of many waters and like the sound of mighty peals of thunder" (Revelation 19:6). John's description indicates that this is a vast, countless host of people, all gathered for the marriage feast of the King's Son, the Lamb of God.

Read and discuss the following hymn stanzas. What connection does the hymn writer make between "the marriage supper of the Lamb" (Revelation 19:9) and Holy Communion?

At the Lamb's high feast we sing
Praise to our victorious King,
Who has washed us in the tide
Flowing from His pierced side. Alleluia!
Praise we Him, whose love divine
Gives His sacred blood for wine,
Gives His body for the feast—
Christ the victim, Christ the priest. Alleluia!

Office hymn, 17th cent.; tr. Robert Campbell, 1814–68, alt. (*LW* 126:1–2)

This joyous Easter hymn draws a connection between "the marriage supper of the Lamb" (Revelation 19:9) and Holy Communion, first by speaking about those who attend the feast as having been "washed" clean in the blood of the Lamb. The connection between image of washing in this hymn stanza and the "fine linen, bright and pure" (Revelation 19:8) is shown by John's earlier words: "These are the ones coming out of the great tribulation. They have washed their robes and made them white in the blood of the Lamb" (Revelation 7:14).

This hymn also uses Revelation 19:6–9 as a description of Holy Communion by stating that we sing "at the Lamb's high feast," praising the one who "gives His sacred blood for wine, gives His body for the feast."

As with John 6 and with other passages from the Scriptures, some Bible scholars might argue that Revelation 9:6–9 is not a reference to Holy Communion. Other scholars would disagree, seeing in this passage strong connections to Holy Communion. At the very least, we can observe that the images and words of Revelation 9:6–9 bring Holy Communion to mind, allowing us to draw a parallel for us between the Lord's Supper (which we celebrate in this life) and the great "feast" of eternal life in heaven.

Revelation 22:1–5 describes another great, heavenly scene. What does it mean that the tree of life yielded its fruit each month (Revelation 22:2)?

Described here is a wonderful scene of ongoing nourishment, health, and satisfaction of hunger. Never again to "hunger and thirst for righteousness" (Matthew 5:6), the people of God find nourishment in "the tree of life" (compare Genesis 2:9 and 3:24). Unlike earthly fruit trees, which bear fruit only once per year, this tree will never be out of season. It will continually provide the saints of God with their nourishment.

Just as the waters of the living stream were open to all the inhabitants, so also the fruits of these trees of life were accessible to all those that lived in the heavenly city. There would never be a lack of fruit, some of it always being in season on account of the fact that a new crop ripened every month. The very leaves of these wonderful tress would have their value; for they would serve for the healing of the nations assembled in the heavenly city, to keep them forever happy and contented in true heavenly bliss. This indicates that we shall be nourished spiritually in the home above, that our heavenly life and our salvation will be sustained and increased by the very richest of gifts of God's grace. We shall have an abundance of heavenly blessings and yet desire ever more of the love of our Lord and Savior Jesus Christ. That, truly, will be life in the word's fullest and truest sense. (Popular Commentary, *p. 654)*

Conclusion

Christians gather at the Lord's Table to take part in the miraculous meal of His body and blood, given for their forgiveness and salvation. Individually they come, but before the Lord they stand as the one, unified, seamless body of Christ (the Church) that extends from age to age. Holy Communion anticipates the festivities and joys of the Last Day, when God's saints shall see with unveiled eyes the very salvation that Holy Communion delivered to them. No longer shall they hunger; no longer shall they thirst. As in the days of the exodus, all the people of God shall eat, drink, and see God.

Closing Prayer

Dear Savior, we come to Your table at Your gracious invitation to eat and drink Your holy body and blood. Let us find favor in Your eyes to receive this holy sacrament in faith for the salvation of our souls and to the glory of Your holy name; for You live and reign with the Father and the Holy Spirit, one God, now and forever. Amen. (LW, *p.128)*

THE ETERNAL FEAST

FOOD IN REVELATION

Breaking Bread

In **Revelation 2:14,** Jesus rebuked the Christians in the church of Pergamum for tolerating false teachers in their midst. Specifically, what error had become popular in this church? What major sins were associated with this error?

According to **Numbers 25:1–2** and **31:16,** what happened to those who originally tolerated this particular false teacher? What similar threat is made against the Christians of Pergamum in **Revelation 2:16?**

Long before John wrote Revelation, Paul wrote a letter to the Corinthians in which he also discussed food sacrificed to idols. John very well could have had Paul's letter in mind when he was writing **Revelation 2:12–17**. Compare **1 Corinthians 10:14–22.** What gift from God does Paul simultaneously discuss when he addresses the topic of food sacrificed to idols?

Now return to **Revelation 2:12–17**. To those in the church of Pergamum who conquer (that is, who remain faithful to the Word of God), what promise is spoken to them in **Revelation 2:17**? Is this promise spoken only to them? What Old Testament event does this promise call to mind?

What is meant by the word "hidden" in **Revelation 2:17?** To what might the phrase "hidden manna" possibly refer?

Some scholars say that **Revelation 2:17** gives no clear indication that "hidden manna" refers to Holy Communion. Many people say the same thing about **John 6:22–59**. Read through that passage, focusing especially on **verses 35, 48–51**, and **53–58**. Without deciding definitively whether or not this passage is about Holy Communion, is it possible at least to say that Jesus' words here sound similar to those used in Holy Communion, or remind us of Holy Communion?

What do the following two hymn stanzas have to say about **John 6:22–59**?

Now in faith I humbly ponder
Over this surpassing wonder
That the bread of life is boundless
Though the souls it feeds are countless:
With the choicest wine of heaven
Christ's own blood to us is given.
Oh, most glorious consolation,
Pledge and seal of my salvation.

Johann Franck, 1618–77; tr. *Lutheran Book of Worship,* 1978. (*LW* 239:3)

O living Bread from heaven,
How well You feed Your guest!
The gifts that You have given
Have filled my heart with rest.
Oh, wondrous food of blessing,
Oh, cup that heals our woes!
My heart, this gift possessing,
With praises overflows.

Johann Rist, 1606–67; tr. Catherine Winkworth, 1829–78, alt. (*LW* 244:1)

The Great Feast

Take a look at **Revelation 3:20**. Some Christians misuse this verse by claiming that, before we can be saved, we must first open up our heart and ask Jesus to come in. What clues can you spot in **Revelation 3:14–21** that suggest that this passage is *not* speaking about God's gift of conversion?

What surprising application of **Revelation 3:20** is made in the following stanza of "Soul Adorn Yourself with Gladness," drawn from the section on the Lord's Supper in *Lutheran Worship*?

Hasten as a bride to meet Him,
Eagerly and gladly greet Him.
There he stands already knocking;
Quickly, now, your gate unlocking,
Open wide the fast-closed portal,
Saying to the Lord immortal:
"Come, and leave your loved one never;
Dwell within My heart forever."

Johann Franck, 1618–77; tr. *Lutheran Book of Worship,* 1978. (*LW* 239:2)

Read **Revelation 19:6–9**. What great event is described here? Who is included in this event?

Bible scholars have noted that Matthew's Gospel was the most popular and widely used Gospel in the Early Church. It is likely that John was familiar with Matthew's Gospel before he wrote Revelation. John may even have had Matthew's Gospel in mind when he wrote **Revelation 19:6–9** in particular. Compare **verse 9** to **Matthew 22:1–14.** According to **verses 9–10** of the Matthew passage, who is invited to the Bridegroom's feast? Comparing Revelation 19:6, how many are included in this great invitation?

Read and discuss the following hymn stanzas. What connection does the hymn writer make between "the marriage supper of the Lamb" (**Revelation 19:9**) and Holy Communion?

At the Lamb's high feast we sing
Praise to our victorious king,
Who has washed us in the tide
Flowing from His pierced side. Alleluia!

Praise we Him, whose love divine
Gives His sacred blood for wine,
Gives His body for the feast—
Christ the victim, Christ the priest. Alleluia!

Office hymn, 17th cent.; tr. Robert Campbell, 1814–68, alt.
(*LW* 126:1–2)

Revelation 22:1–5 describes another great, heavenly scene. What does it mean that the tree of life yielded its fruit each month (**Revelation 22:2**)?

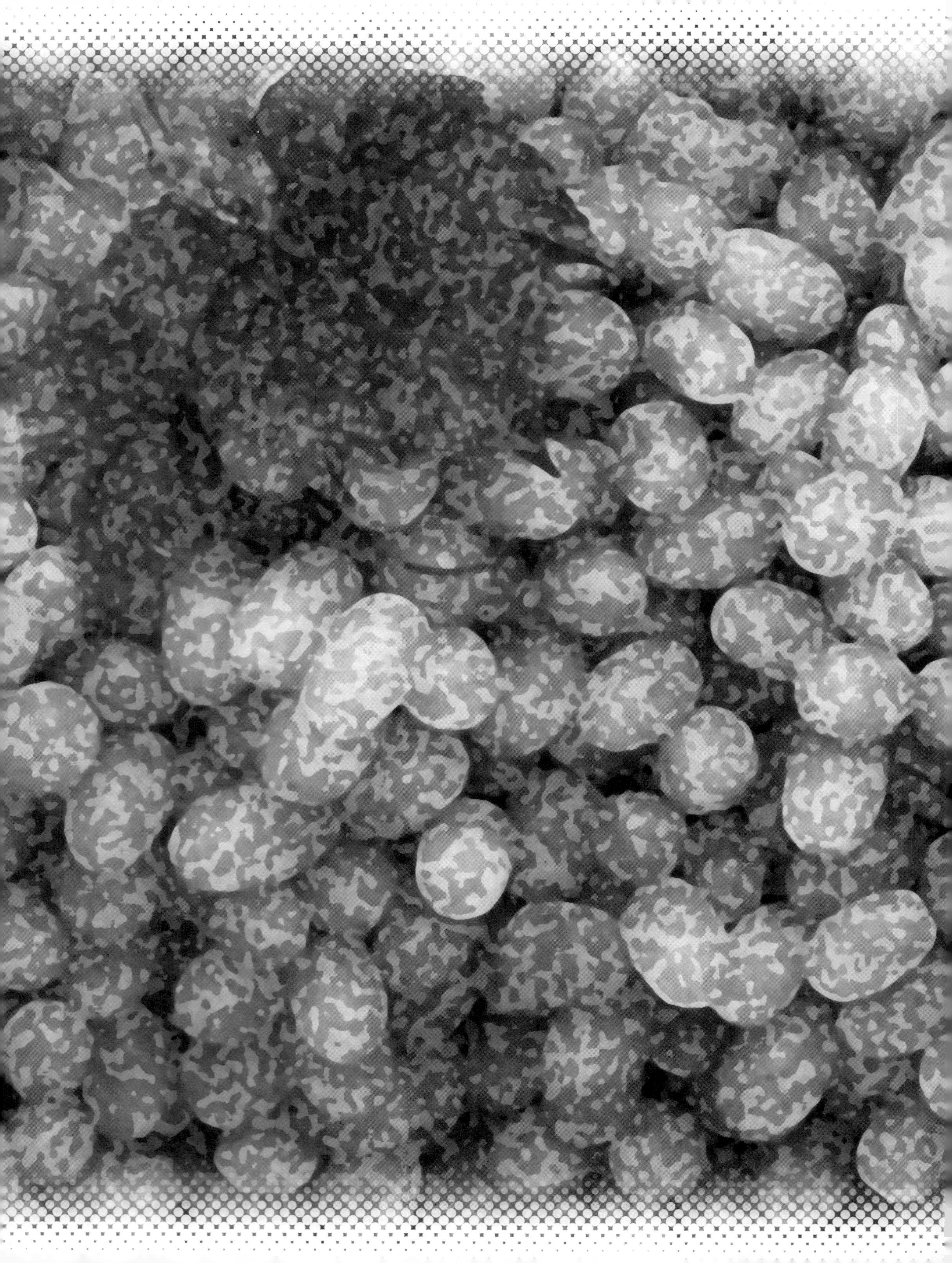